BEYOND THE
NUCLEAR FREEZE

BOOKS BY ROBERT F. DRINAN

Religion, the Courts and Public Policy, 1963
Democracy, Dissent & Disorder, 1969
Vietnam and Armageddon, 1970
The Right to Be Educated (editor), 1968
Honor the Promise—America's Commitment to Israel, 1977

BEYOND THE
NUCLEAR FREEZE

ROBERT F. DRINAN, S.J.

The Seabury Press / New York

Second printing

1983
The Seabury Press
815 Second Avenue
New York, N.Y. 10017

Copyright © 1983 by Robert F. Drinan

Printed in the United States of America

Library of Congress Cataloging in Publication Data

Drinan, Robert F.
  Beyond the nuclear freeze.
  Bibliography: p.
  Includes index.
  1. United States—Military policy. 2. Antinuclear movement—United States. 3. Arms race—History—20th century. 4. Atomic warfare—Religious aspects—Christianity. 5. Atomic warfare—Moral and ethical aspects. 6. World politics—1975–1985. 7. Catholic Church—Doctrinal and controversial works—Catholic authors. I. Title.
UA23.D7   1983   355'.0335'73   83-427
ISBN: 0-814-2406-3 (pbk.)

Contents

ONE / The Origin of the Nuclear Freeze Movement   1

TWO / The Explosion in Sales of Conventional Weapons   8

THREE / The United States Introduces the Nuclear Age   20

FOUR / Arms Control in the Generation after Hiroshima   32

FIVE / Carter and SALT II: Reagan and START   51

SIX / Congress and the Nuclear Freeze in 1982   65

SEVEN / Should the United States Renounce the First Use
of Nuclear Weapons?   79

EIGHT / Are Nuclear Weapons Illegal?   89

NINE / Is Nuclear Deterrence Immoral in Catholic Tradition?   99

TEN / The Urgency of Understanding the Russians   119

ELEVEN / Can Catastrophe Be Averted?   131

Bibliography   161

Index   163

one

The Origin of the Nuclear Freeze Movement

The fright and fear about nuclear war that humanity has experienced since 1945 deepened acutely in the early 1980s. The thought that the United States might again use the bomb became unbearable for countless Americans. Europeans trembled because the Soviets were launching fourth-generation intercontinental ballistic missiles at the rate of more than one hundred per year. Europeans were also concerned about U.S. officials stating that a nuclear war was "winnable."

On June 15, 1982 the USSR announced at the United Nations that it would continue to renounce the first use of nuclear weapons. On July 11, 1982, in an unusual full-page article in *Pravda*, the Kremlin detailed the reasons why the Soviet government is convinced that the United States is engaging in actions that "are aimed at creating prerequisites for a struggle to destroy socialism as a sociopolitical system." As the means to achieve this end the article specifically mentioned neutron bombs, the MX intercontinental missile, the B-1 long-range bomber, and Cruise missiles. The *Pravda* article suggested a shift in Soviet thinking toward the use of a policy of "launch on warning"—a system by which nuclear missiles would be triggered almost automatically if an enemy attack were detected. Such a policy would, of course, be dangerous because it raises the specter of nuclear devastation triggered by a human or computer malfunction along the lines of several accidents of this nature in the United States military.

The fears of millions of citizens in the West about the possibility of nuclear war were intensified by the increasing knowledge of nuclear power that the ordinary person almost had forced on him. Physicians for Social Responsibility, a group of medical doctors long devoted to raising consciousness about nuclear warfare, continued an intensive campaign to focus on the appalling medical consequences of the exploding of even one atomic bomb. Lawyers concerned with the dangers of the atomic bomb proposed legal reasons why nuclear warfare was arguably already a violation of the rules of war set forth in the treaties and conventions of Geneva and The Hague. Religious groups, sensing a new receptivity to the moral dimensions of the problem, launched activities to involve all believers in what clearly by everyone's admission is the primordial moral and religious problem of the age.

On November 18, 1981, the 300 Catholic bishops issued a lengthy statement condemning virtually every single use of the nuclear weapon. This declaration, to be discussed at length later in this book, constitutes possibly the most rigorously argued and comprehensively stated pronouncement of any religious body on nuclear warfare in the nearly forty years since the existence of the nuclear bomb became the most intractable, horrifying, and unbearable problem that humanity has to confront.

No one really knows why it took almost two generations before the nuclear freeze movement was able to produce seven hundred thousand persons in New York City on June 12, 1982—the largest demonstration in American history. Nor is it clear why there was a dramatic convergence of forces in the early 1980s on the nuclear war. In Europe the scheduled introduction in 1983 of 572 medium-range Pershing II rockets to the NATO nations prompted unprecedented fears. It was this development, among many others, that gave birth to the words in the appeal for European nuclear disarmament in April 1980: "We must commence to act as if a united, neutral and pacific Europe exists. We must learn to be loyal, not to 'East' or 'West' but to each other."

In the United States the Reagan administration clearly shifted the tone if not the substance of America's intentions toward Russia. And the wars in El Salvador, the Falklands, and Lebanon, as well as the battles between Iran and Iraq, all contributed to the deepening feeling of people everywhere that nuclear weapons are just too dangerous to have around.

Lawrence Freedman in a 1981 comprehensive 400-page book, *The Evolution of Nuclear Strategy,* summed up well the anxiety about nuclear weapons in these words: "An international order that rests upon a stability created by nuclear weapons will be the most terrible legacy with which each succeeding generation will endow the next. To believe that this can go on indefinitely without major disaster requires an optimism unjustified by any historical or political perspective."

Perhaps the factor that most contributed to the explosion of protest about the nuclear bomb was the increase in information about what the United States and its adversary were doing in building up nuclear arsenals. Prior to the early 1980s both the experts and the nonexperts on nuclear weapons practically made a pact that even the best-informed citizens did not have to learn about megatonnage, the ICBMs, Backfire bombers, or even the triad. As information about these and related topics trickled down, the American public began to realize to their astonishment the horrifying predicament in which their nation was trapped. Citizens had been chagrined and surprised over the unbelievably inept way in which their government handled the war in Vietnam. Citizens had also been humiliated over Watergate—the greatest political scandal in American history. But in the early 1980s they began to realize that they had to face another awful spectacle—the nuclear arms race—a situation created and perpetuated by U.S. planners and politicians who did their work, as in the Vietnam and Watergate fiascoes, secretly and with little accountability.

The information that people somehow began to grasp in the early 1980s related, for example, to the navy and its development of strategic missiles. The story is simple. But as one absorbs it, one can understand the dread and terror in the Soviet Union at the possibility of a first-strike attack by U.S. submarine-launched ballistic missiles (SLBMs).

The first SLBM, the Polaris, carried a single warhead. It could strike targets at a distance of 1,200 nautical miles with a probable error of a mile or two. The Polaris was soon upgraded to carry three warheads and travel 2,500 nautical miles with probable error of about 3,000 feet. The Poseidon replaced the Polaris and has the capacity of dropping ten warheads within 1,800 feet of their target. The Trident I, the most advanced missile in the navy arsenal, has a range of 4,000 nautical miles and improved accuracy, but still lacks the combination of accuracy and payload needed to destroy targets hardened with steel and concrete, such as missile silos and command centers. Trident II, now in an accelerated period of development, will predictably be able to destroy the Soviet Union's primary strategic force, its land-based intercontinental missiles. In addition, Trident II could be fired from submarines near the Soviet coast, thus giving far less warning time than the flight of land-based missiles from the United States.

Some arms controllers fear that Trident II will increase the likelihood of nuclear war. Herbert Scoville, Jr., for example, president of the Arms Control Association and a former deputy director of the CIA, has stated that Trident II is "a step backward" and that it will be destabilizing because it will provide an incentive to Soviet leaders to prepare to launch a retaliatory attack more automatically. Other experts consider Trident II preferable to land-based missiles, which are easier for the Soviets to target.

In the early 1980s Americans, becoming aware of all of the implications of the development of Trident II and closely related events, cried out almost in panic. The only thing on which these Americans could agree was the plea for a nuclear freeze. It was more a "cri de coeur" than a plan or program from the mind. It was almost like the cry of a student who has been missing class and does not understand the lesson for today. The cry for a nuclear freeze did not, however, naively recommend that America unilaterally disarm or go back to the world before Hiroshima and Nagasaki. It pleaded only for *some* explanation, *some* justification, *some* understandable rationale for America's nuclear policy. The nuclear freeze movement was in essence a plea from the people for a role in the arms-control dialogue, from which they felt excluded.

Where will the arms-control or freeze movement go? In 1983 it is impossible to predict. Seeing the complexity of the issues involved, the depths of fear that the United States has always had for communism, and the possibility that other problems and issues might capture the imagination of citizens in the West, it is not impossible that the outburst of anger and the demonstrations of anguish might again be subdued or silenced. The lack of clear, relatively short-range and attainable political objectives is another reason why the nuclear freeze movement might evaporate or at least become quiescent.

But what is certain is that the present moment is a time of unparalleled opportunity and challenge. Religious persons would say that a grace has come from God to illuminate the minds and inspire the hearts of those who feel guilt at their complicity in a role that is strange and new for an America that, until the cold war began, never before declared itself a permanent adversary of any nation in the world. Other persons would say that they want relief from the haunting burden of thinking that they, by their inaction, might permit their children to be incinerated and the whole world to be almost annihilated by a nuclear holocaust.

The moment is also propitious for nuclear arms control in that the strategic strength of both sides is at the moment roughly equivalent. It would seem, moreover, that even a major effort by one side or the other could not easily upset the balance for some time to come.

No one should minimize the importance of the nuclear freeze movement. It will be derided by hard-liners as incoherent, naive, leaderless, and without a focus. But the fact remains that the broad-based grass-roots movement to outlaw nuclear war that came together more or less around the time that the Reagan administration came to power may well become one of the most powerful movements in the whole history of mankind.

What should the members of that movement know? Some of what they should know is covered in this book. First there is a history and an analysis of the worldwide surge in recent years in the purchase of conventional weapons—purchases that now total an unbelievable $550 billion per year. It should be noted that even though the whole world is distressed and depressed over the possibility of a nuclear holocaust, the escalating sale of conventional arms almost inevitably means that there will be an increasing number of nonnuclear wars.

Persons anxious to bring about a nuclear freeze are often impatient with the results and the process by which SALT I and SALT II came about. They have reason to be. In November 1969, on the eve of the first SALT talks, the United States had roughly 2,300 warheads, the Soviet Union 1,400. After a decade of arms negotiation in the SALT process those figures now stand at 7,500 warheads apiece. Despite these disappointments, the fact is that the SALT process is the major way by which the superpowers communicate about nuclear weapons. There are all types of reasons to believe that consciousness raising outside the SALT process is essential. But there are equally compelling reasons why the "freezeniks" and everyone alarmed by the arms race should be completely knowledgeable about SALT, or the Strategic Arms Reduction Talks (START), as President Reagan has renamed them.

If those interested in arms control are disillusioned with the tedious and tormenting pace of the SALT process, they can receive at least a limited amount of encouragement from the accomplishments of the nuclear nonproliferation treaty agreed to in 1968. If American-Soviet negotiations have been unsatisfactory in constraining the level of arms between them, they have nonetheless exercised a powerful influence worldwide, so that at least in part as a result of their efforts the number of actual powers with nuclear weapons now comes to only six.

Perhaps the most encouraging development in the entire dreary story of failure in arms control is the success that the nations of the earth have had, at least until the past year or so, in agreeing to a ban on chemical and biological warfare. If the nations can do this, the question keeps recurring, Why can they not agree to ban nuclear weapons, which are thousands of times more devastating than chemical or biological instruments of destruction?

If the nuclear menace is to be controlled, clearly a deep belief and a profound adherence to moral values will be essential. For that reason the deepening involvement of European and American churches in issues related to nuclear war may have a significance that strengthens and transcends the participation of academics, physicians, lawyers, and all who are tormented by the nuclear threat. Hence, the position that religious groups have taken—especially the Catholic bishops of the United States and Europe—will be thoroughly reviewed.

There is no one clear way by which the threatened nuclear holocaust can be prevented. But recommendations as to approach for attitudes and conduct will be made in the last chapter based on a balanced evaluation of all of the scientific, military, moral, and political aspects of a problem that, it is not an exaggeration to say, is the hardest and most urgent that mankind has ever had to confront.

two

The Explosion in Sales of Conventional Weapons

In 1982 the nations of the earth spent about $550 billion on arms and armament. In 1960 the total was $100 billion. The 1982 figure comes to an average of $110 for each of the 4.2 billion persons on earth.

Pope John Paul II, in a statement read by Cardinal Agostino Casaroli to the United Nations General Assembly's Special Session on Disarmament on June 11, 1982, noted that "for many inhabitants of this planet that [sum of $110] represents the income available to them for maintaining life over the same period." The Pope went on to state that "the nations of the earth are already overarmed and far too committed to policies reenforcing this tendency." He added that "the production of conventional arms throughout the world is a really alarming phenomenon."

It seems self-evident that the earth's 167 countries are spending more on weapons for war than in any previous age of mankind. The 1982 study, *Common Security—A Blueprint for Survival*, issued by the independent Commission on Disarmament and Security Issues, of which Cyrus Vance was a member, reported that "world military expenditure is more than 12 times as great in real terms as it was 50 years ago; it is more than 28 times as great as it was in 1908."

The past decade, moreover, saw an incredible escalation in the acquisition of arms. The U.S. Arms Control and Disarmament Agency (ACDA) states that for 1979 the developing nations spent $129 billion on defense, triple the cost of a decade earlier. With adjustments for inflation, Africa's arms imports in 1979 cost eleven times what they did a decade earlier. Arms imports in Latin America during the same period were up 608 percent.

The explosion of armament costs has many causes. Developing nations like Pakistan have an understandable fear of invasion—by India on one side and the USSR by way of Afghanistan on the other. Saudi Arabia was so convinced that it was militarily vulnerable that it pressured the Reagan White House to force through a reluctant Senate a measure to permit the sale of $8.5 billion for AWACS aircraft, Sidewinder missiles, aerial tankers, and fuel tanks for F-15 fighter aircraft.

But one of the central forces that induces so many nations to cripple their economies and impose sacrifices on their people is the powerful attraction of becoming a client state of the Soviet Union or of the United States. The sale of weapons has now become the prime instrument used by both superpowers in their rivalry for the allegiance of the Third World. Economic aid has declined but military assistance has grown.

Over the past decade the United States has provided weapons and military services totaling more than $123 billion to about 130 of the world's nations. In 1981 President Reagan recommended to Congress arms sales totaling over $25 billion—surpassing by a wide margin those of any previous year in American history.

In 1981 the United States approved for the first time the sale of lethal military equipment to the People's Republic of China. In the same year the White House approved the first sale of highly advanced jet aircraft to any Latin American country when it cleared for Venezuela a sale of $615 million for twenty-four F-16 fighter aircraft. At the same time a $1.1 billion deal with Pakistan for forty F-16s won approbation.

The explosion of arms sales in the early 1980s was preceded by a steady skyrocketing of such transactions in earlier decades. Throughout the 1950s and 1960s the vast majority of U.S. weapons exports were made free of charge to the recipients. In the early 1970s the strengthening of the economies of U.S. allies and the strain on the U.S. budget as a result of the war in Vietnam led to a shift, so that most arms were transferred for cash or for credit. Under the new setup the United States foreign cash sales jumped from $3 billion in 1972 to $16 billion in 1975. During the same period U.S. military aid fell from $4 billion to $1.9 billion.

Foreign military transactions involving the United States in the 1970s totaled $77.9 billion. In 1974 the Congress, concerned over the expanding arms trade, enacted the Arms Export Control Act, permitting the sale of military equipment over $25 million to be vetoed by a majority vote of both houses. The Congress has never succeeded in blocking a single sale; in 1981 the $25 million ceiling was lifted to $50 million.

President Carter came to office pledging to reduce the amount of U.S. arms transfers. The Carter administration rejected over $1 billion in requests for arms from some sixty nations and cut off or reduced military assistance to a dozen regimes deemed to be consistent and gross violators of human rights.

But the global momentum behind the arms race prevented the Carter administration from abiding by its resolve to diminish the international traffic in arms. After a small drop in 1977, the export of American weapons rose from $10.1 billion in the mid-1970s to a new high of $17.4 billion in 1980. Some $40 billion in arms were sold to the Third World during the Carter administration and an additional $55 billion backlog of undelivered orders was left for the Reagan White House to process.

President Carter's intentions were, however, admirable. In

May 1977 he said: ''The United States will henceforth view arms transfers as an exceptional foreign policy instrument, to be used only in circumstances where it can be clearly demonstrated that the transfer contributes to our security and the security of our close friends.''

This policy is in sharp contrast with the following statement of President Reagan in July 1981: ''The United States therefore views the transfer of conventional arms . . . as an essential element of its global defense posture and an indispensable component of its foreign policy.''

Pursuant to the Reagan policy the value of foreign military sales proposed by President Reagan in his first year of office rose to $25.3 billion. In addition, the outright military aid approved by the Congress for fiscal year 1982 came to $4.7 billion—more than four times the sum of $1.1 billion appropriated for 1981.

The creation by the Reagan administration of a warehouse for weapons further institutionalized the role of the United States as the number-one supplier of arms in the world. The establishment in 1981 of the Special Defense Acquisition Fund created a fund for fiscal year 1983 of $600 million. This measure created a stockpile of those weapons most likely to be requested by other governments. This development makes the United States capable of rushing arms anywhere in the world where a conflict breaks out. The very existence of this new stockpile arguably makes it easier to yield promptly to the request of a nation confronted by what it conceives to be an external or domestic threat.

The promotion of arms sales by the United States clearly invites and encourages developing nations to employ their resources on armaments. The slowing or undermining of development programs is inevitable. By the same process the United States creates permanent client states dependent politically and psychologically on the United States for spare parts, bank loans, and military strategists.

The theory, of course, behind the massive arms sales is to counter communism by making allies of those who purchase their weapons from the United States. But, up to the time of the

Carter administration, aid and sales had been extended to twenty-eight of the forty-one military-dominated governments in the world with records of violating the rights of citizens by arbitrary arrest, torture, and summary execution. In the past two decades the United States exported almost $27 billion worth of arms to these twenty-eight countries and over the past three decades has trained 347,000 military personnel from those lands.

The facts about arms sales by the USSR are almost as impressive or frightening as those of the United States. Figures provided by the Congressional Research Service (CRS) show that in the years 1976–80 Soviet agreements to sell arms totaled $42.8 billion, compared with $49.7 billion for the United States. The Reagan administration testified in 1981 that in 1977–80 Soviet deliveries of arms to the Third World exceeded those of the United States by 20 percent. Although this estimate may be open to question, the CRS data do show that in 1980 Soviet arms agreements totaled $14.9 billion, compared with $9.7 billion for the United States.

The total sales for noncommunist nations were, however, much higher, since France is the world's third largest supplier after the United States and the USSR. Britain is number four, while Germany and Italy annually export large quantities of arms.

The CRS estimates that in 1980 noncommunist nations entered into arms-transfer agreements with the Third World worth $25 billion, compared with $15 billion for the Soviet Union.

The permanent impact of the importation of sophisticated weapons by the Third World can be seen in the evidence set forth by Andrew J. Pierre in *The Global Politics of Arms Sales*. He notes that in 1960 only four developing nations had supersonic combat aircraft. By 1977 the number had risen to forty-seven. The same proliferation has occurred with respect to long-range surface-to-air missiles, going from two countries in 1960 to twenty-seven in the mid-1970s.

Anthony Sampson, the English author and specialist on arms sales, has written that today's massive arms sales are the "blind spot of a generation.'' He suggested that every generation has its own blind spot, which is incomprehensible to future generations. He compares massive sales of weapons to the purchases of slaves in the 1800s and the employment of children as laborers in the early 1900s. But, unlike those now discontinued evils, the presence of massive numbers of weapons around the world is likely to have consequences the horror of which can now hardly be imagined. Even if, as predicted by some, arms sales fall off as nations reach the saturation point, the very existence of highly developed military equipment all around the world will tend to produce wars. Regional rivalries will be created or inflamed. Weapons will be used to perpetuate an authoritarian regime or to overthrow a military dictatorship. Even worse, weapons of all kinds will be acquired by theft or by purchase by terrorists of all ideological descriptions. In short, the widespread existence of weapons can be compared to the existence of vast quantities of poisons capable of producing pestilences or plagues like those in the Dark Ages, which killed thousands, even millions of people.

In the early 1980s the worldwide near frenzy for a nuclear freeze revealed that people everywhere were alarmed at the hideous potential of the world's 50,000 nuclear weapons. No comparable revulsion is visible over the existence of a vast arsenal of conventional weapons unprecedented in human history. The four major suppliers—the United States, the USSR, France, and Britain—accounted for 87.5 percent of the weapons transfers to the Third World. The competition among the major supplying corporations in these four countries and the fear that any lessening of exports would bring about a loss of jobs have combined to perpetuate the wholesale transfer of arms of all kinds.

In 1961 President Eisenhower presciently saw all of this coming. He warned in his farewell broadcast to the nation of an entirely new element in American experience—''the conjunction of an immense military establishment and a large arms industry.'' He felt even then that there was an ''unwarranted influence by the military-industrial complex.'' The last soldier-president urged the nation not to succumb to ''the temptation to feel that some spectacular and costly action could become the miraculous solution to all current difficulties.''

America has clearly pursued the conviction that the nations to whom the United States gives or sells arms will be friends and allies. History, however, does not validate that hope. The United States sold vast quantities of sophisticated arms to Iran. To many Iranians this was seen as strong support for the Shah. To some the Shah was just an American puppet. Hence, the U.S.-made arsenal in Iran did not buy friendship; rather the United States came to be perceived as the number-one enemy of the Iranian people. Indeed, the Iranian seizure of fifty-two American hostages and the subsequent total rejection of the United States has become a dramatic example of the uncertainty of the proposition that a nation can create friends by the sale of arms. In this case the vast amounts of American weaponry sold to Iran were later used in Iran's 1982 invasion of Iraq.

The enormous difficulties inherent in any attempt to reduce the sale of arms become very clear in a review of the intensive efforts of the Carter administration to limit the quantity of arms sales from the United States. In May 1977 the Carter administration issued guidelines with six specific provisions designed, among other things, to prevent the introduction of weapons new to a regime, to deter the transfer of the weapons to third parties without U.S. consent, and to discourage the promotion of the sale of conventional arms. Specialists on arms control have been critical of alleged inconsistencies in the Carter administration's approach to limiting the transfer of arms. But praise is due for the close involvement of the president himself and the genuine if sometimes ineffective attempts to develop an overall policy to control the sale of arms to all countries except the eighteen that are treaty allies of the United States. Inevitably, those who wanted a stricter control criticized the implementation of the Carter policy as one with too many exceptions, while those close to the defense industry looked upon the policy as unworkable and naive. Everyone would probably agree that the Carter White House should have sought more cooperation from England and

France. But the sincerity and intensity of America's first serious attempt to curb the role of the United States as the merchant of death must be commended. At least the Carter policy of restraint looks forceful compared to the permissiveness of the Reagan administration. Early in that regime the under secretary of state for security assistance, science and technology, James Buckley, told the Aerospace Industries Association that the Carter administration had adopted policies on arms sales that "substituted theology for a healthy sense of self-protection." The Reagan administration went on to make the transfer of arms, absent any specific guidelines, one of the key components in its dealings with any noncommunist nation. The Reagan administration asked Congress for the removal of the ban on arms sales for Argentina and Chile, urged the repeal of the Clark Amendment, which prohibits military assistance to the anti-Marxist faction in Angola, and the overturn of the Symington Amendment, which in effect outlawed aid to Pakistan until it pledged to refrain from developing nuclear weapons. The Reagan administration, furthermore, sold Cobra helicopters to Jordan, F-16s to South Korea and Venezuela, lethal weapons to China; the administration also made other transfers of weapons to Somalia, Sudan, Tunisia, and Turkey.

All of this was done of course in the name of facing up to "the realities of Soviet aggrandizement," as Mr. Buckley put it. But what is lacking is any sense of the long-range consequences of permitting dozens of unstable governments to possess the most dangerous kinds of weapons without the United States having any control over their use or transfer.

The problem is obviously not simple. Khrushchev in 1954 began a policy of furnishing arms to new nations in the less developed world. Ever since that time the USSR has made the Third World one of its major battlegrounds in its ideological struggle with the West. The Kremlin deems it to be to its advantage to intervene with arms at least indirectly in regions characterized by unstable situations and weak governments. But the Soviets, like the Americans, have not always been rewarded with lasting friendship for their presentation of weapons. The Soviets transferred $1.2 billion in arms to Sukarno prior to 1965, but even this did not stop the ouster of the Soviets from Indonesia. The Congo, Ghana, and Guinea have been places where Soviet generosity with weapons did not prevent a long series of Soviet failures. Nor did the arms of the USSR prevent China's final break with the Kremlin in 1960 nor, some years later, the expulsion of 17,000 Soviet military personnel from Egypt.

Is there any way by which the four top suppliers of conventional arms can bring about some decrease in the world's $550 billion annual expenditure for the military—80 percent of which is for nonnuclear conventional weapons? The fact is that there have been very few internationally orchestrated attempts to control the traffic in guns. The massive sales go on largely invisible to all but specialists in the arms-control community. But again the possibility of wars being triggered or regional conflicts initiated by a profusion of conventional arms is probably much more likely than by the presence of nuclear bombers. Similarly, the risk of terrorists threatening blackmail would appear to be much more likely to occur with conventional weapons than with a nuclear bomb. Despite all of this, the acute dangers that could arise from the very presence of arsenals in widely differing countries of the world have not yet entered the popular imagination.

There is not even a method of consultation between the United States and its European allies on arms sales to the Third World. NATO has always considered this issue to be outside of its charter. Nor is there any mechanism among the Western powers to discuss arms sales to China. Sales to Peking are not discussed with Moscow, although few problems can be imagined to be as sensitive to the Western-Chinese-Soviet relationship in the 1980s.

During the 1970s American and British officials discussed at the Geneva Conference on Disarmament the desirability of curtailing arms sales. In 1976 Secretary of State Kissinger proposed in essence that the recipient states should assume the burden of establishing regional arrangements to regulate weapons sales. The only regional attempt to date to do so was the Declaration of Ayacucho in 1974 by which eight Latin American Andean nations committed themselves to create conditions that would permit effective limitations on the acquisition of weapons for offensive purposes. But this declaration did not prevent sizable arms purchases by Chile, Ecuador, and Peru. The restraints by the recipients were not respected by the suppliers, because after 1974 the USSR sold advanced fighters to Peru and France sold Mirage fighters to Ecuador.

The Carter administration's efforts to control and curtail traffic in conventional arms stand as the most ambitious, even though ultimately not entirely successful, attempts to restrain arms transfers. In March 1977 Secretary of State Vance's proposals on SALT II proferred in Moscow were rejected, but agreement was obtained to set up a bilateral working group on arms transfers. American and Soviet delegations met four times in 1977 and 1978. The story of those meetings is recorded by Leslie Gelb, director of the State Department's Bureau of Politico-Military Affairs, in the September 1980 issue of *Arms Control Today*. Internal differences between personnel of the Carter administration contributed to the breakdown of the talks, but the absence of the two major European suppliers from the discussions also contributed to their failure.

Clearly the uncoordinated sale of massive military equipment to new and often unstable nations of the Third World is contrary to the political interests of the West. Only the suppliers can effectively evolve some sort of a policy as to when Western nations should furnish helicopters, armored vehicles, naval vessels, and other such equipment. The haphazard arms bazaar now available to any nation that can buy is an invitation to disaster.

No one says that serious, good-faith negotiations on this topic with the Soviets will be easy. But the Kremlin might at least make some concessions if it could obtain commitments that the Western powers and Japan would not furnish weapons to the People's Republic of China. Perhaps the Soviets could be persuaded to stay out of Latin America in return for some concessions useful to them.

The Third World nations understand the dangerous situations that are arising as a result of the unrestrained flow of arms from the USSR and from Britain, France, and the United States. In 1978 at the UN Special Session on Disarmament the nonaligned nations modified their position and supported this statement in the final document: "Consulation should be carried out among major arms supplier and recipient countries on the limitation of all types of international transfers of conventional weapons, based in particular on the principle of undiminished security of the parties with a view to promoting or enhancing stability at a lower military level."

It is unrealistic to think that the nations in the Third World that are developing into major powers will forgo completely the possession of those ever more expensive jets and tanks that air force and army leaders all around the world deem essential to their profession.

The race for superiority or at least parity in conventional weapons on the part of the non-Western nations will continue—intensified, no doubt, by the huckstering of the arms merchants of the developed nations. The total overall picture is frightening. Two superpowers are at war in the Third World. Moscow provides military support for allies and friends in North Vietnam, Syria, Iraq, Somalia, Cuba, and elsewhere. The United States ships arms to El Salvador, Israel, Australia, South Korea, and dozens of other nations in every part of the globe.

Who is responsible for this insane arms buildup? There is plenty of blame to go around. America is not the only guilty party. But at least we can ask why the United States has not been insisting at home and abroad that the United States must get out of its role of establishing arsenals of weapons in every corner of the globe. With the exception of President Carter, no president since the arms race began in the late 1940s has done anything but condone it. If all of the religious, social, and political groups that support the nuclear freeze turned their anger and their scorn at America's really horrifying role as the world's number-one supplier of the instruments of death and destruction, we might witness a major modification of America's policy on arms sales, just as we have seen a new attention and possibly a real change in the Reagan administration as a result of the protests against nuclear war by millions on both sides of the Atlantic. If the nuclear bomb is ticking, the explosions that can be anticipated from the global proliferation of conventional weapons cannot be far behind.

three

The United States Introduces the Nuclear Age

The process by which the United States, in the name of national security and world peace, has diffused conventional weapons all around the world contains perhaps some elements of truth and logic. At least it is more justifiable than the policy by which the United States has in readiness 30,000 nuclear weapons in its triad of land, sea, and air nuclear installations. The process by which this system evolved over a period of almost forty years has been the subject of hundreds of books. But no matter how much one reads, the buildup of nuclear weapons does not become any more comprehensible or justifiable. It is a situation beyond control and out of control. It is one of the horror stories of American and world history. Its resolution will require every ounce of moral energy that the United States has ever possessed. A failure to resolve it may mean that history will record that the United States, one of the most idealistic of all nations, will turn out to be history's greatest malefactor of humanity.

It is not easy for any American to recognize the primary responsibility that the United States has for the nuclear weapon. It was the United States that developed the bomb—not necessarily for use in World War II but to counter Germany, which in the early 1940s was reportedly developing the nuclear weapon. Alone among nations, the United States detonated two nuclear weapons in an attack against an enemy country.

For almost forty years most Americans have been trying to deny responsibility or to mitigate culpability for the bombing of Hiroshima and Nagasaki. I have never understood how or why history has been so kind to President Truman in the light of his role as the only leader in all of human history who made the decision to use nuclear weapons. In an extensive analysis of every approach to the morality of war ever set forth in the Judeo-Christian tradition, I have not found any rationale that would justify what was done at Hiroshima and Nagasaki. The usual explanation is that if the bombing had not occurred, an invasion of Japan by up to one million American soldiers would have been necessary. This attempted explanation does not square with the facts. Japan in early August 1945 was near collapse.

It has become clear, moreover, that an agreement had been made among the allies at the Yalta Conference in February 1945 that the Soviet Union would enter the war against Japan in early August. In view of this situation the secretary of war, Mr. Henry Stimson, years after the bombings, wrote that the use of atomic bombs was not to shorten the agony of war, as President Truman had asserted, but "to get a political advantage in the United States' postwar strategy against the Soviet Union."

One has to conclude that the bombings on Hiroshima on August 6, 1945, and on Nagasaki three days later were ordered only partly because of a weariness with the war. Anger at the Japanese also entered in. But the awful question keeps recurring: Would the United States have benefited all of humanity if it had refrained from the use of the nuclear weapon? Would all of history have been changed? Would the United States now be considered the redeemer of mankind rather than the nation that, by its role in developing and detonating the first nuclear weapon, has introduced to the world a scourge worse than any set of evils that humanity has ever been required to confront?

President Truman never expressed regret at what he did, but in 1982 newly discovered papers of his revealed that in 1958 he expressed concern that the world might soon end in a nuclear war. He proposed that the United Nations form "an international police force" to maintain peace. In the hitherto unpublished memorandum Truman wrote: "Now we are faced with total destruction. The old Hebrew prophets presented the idea of the destruction of the world by fire . . . that destruction is at hand unless the great leaders of the world prevent it."

Truman said that he saw the world "faced with a situation that means either total destruction" or "the greatest age in history."

It may be that the absence of guilt on Truman's part is one of the reasons for the lack of very much articulated shame by the American people at the use of the nuclear weapon by the United States. The absence of guilt is one of the reasons why a bill proposed in Congress for several years that would permit a few of the four hundred thousand persons burned and injured in Japan to acquire medical treatment in the United States has never passed. Nations, like individuals, are good at suppressing their guilt, just as Americans have virtually forgotten the vast misery in Vietnam caused by the American bombardments. Reparations agreed to in the Paris Accords have never been given. Nowhere has there been any substantial outcry in the United States to fulfill this commitment—a pledge that the United States government says has been abrogated because Hanoi has taken over South Vietnam.

If the United States felt profound regret, shame, and guilt over the death and destruction caused in Hiroshima and Nagasaki, would the ban-the-bomb movement have a good deal more support? The answer has to be yes. But it is still uncertain whether the American people are moving toward a new conviction that the nation did something truly horrible and unjustifiable on August 6 and 9, 1945. The adherents of the nuclear freeze movement specialize in portraying as dramatically as possible what was done at Hiroshima and Nagasaki, but the accent is on the tragedies that would result from further detonations rather than the shame and guilt that mankind and especially Americans should feel over the thousands killed in the aftermath of the two nuclear weapons used to conclude World War II.

Some might argue that, after all, between March and August of 1945 conventional air attacks of unmatched ferocity on Tokyo, Osaka, Kobe, Yokohama, and fifty-eight secondary Japanese cities with a total population of 6.5 million caused the deaths of 250,000 Japanese along with some 450,000 civilian casualties. Those who want to minimize the impact of the nuclear weapons might also cite the fact that more than 100,000 persons are thought to have died in the saturation bombing of Dresden in February 1945. To the contention that the nuclear weapons were not qualitatively different from the massive destruction caused by conventional weapons, one can only answer that the nuclear assault on Hiroshima and Nagasaki was different because it unleashed physical forces that have made the era after the first mushroom cloud different from any period in the entire history of mankind.

The surge of opposition to nuclear war in the early 1980s dramatized long-dormant recollections of what the bombs did to the people of Japan.

In any assessment of what a nuclear weapon would do now one must preface the description of the bomb's explosion by stating that there is actually no way to really know what it would be like. The bombs available today are many times more powerful than those used at Hiroshima and Nagasaki. And we still find it difficult to comprehend what happened there. But, nonetheless, mankind now understands at least in part that within five years of the nuclear explosion in Hiroshima 200,000 people died. Within the same period of time the death rate at Nagasaki rose to 140,000. The death rate in both cities continues to rise as long-term effects such as cancer manifest themselves. At periodic intervals, as victims succumb to leukemia and other sicknesses relating to the explosion at Hiroshima, the total number of deaths from the long-term effects of the blast is posted. In August 1982 it was 100,717.

The world has now understood that it would be impossible to give even basic medical care to the victims of nuclear attack. John Hersey told the story in 1946 in *Hiroshima:* "Of 150 doctors, 65 were already dead and most of the rest were wounded; of 1780 nurses, 1654 were dead or too badly hurt to work. In the biggest hospital, that of the Red Cross, only 6 doctors out of 30 were able to function, and only 10 nurses out of more than 200."

The literature about the effects of the bomb continues to appear. One of the most reliable studies was issued in 1978 by the U.S. Office of Technology Assessment (OTA). The first effect of the nuclear weapon is a flash of intense white light strong enough to blind observers several miles away. The heat that comes from the fireball reaches 10 million degrees centigrade. Any person within three miles of the fireball will be killed by the heat alone. The heat and light are followed by a blast wave pursued by hurricane-force winds strong enough to overturn trucks and crush buildings. The fireball turns into a mushroom cloud, a massive gathering together of radioactive atoms that will be scattered over a wide area. Harmful radioactive materials will be carried thousands of miles, so that for decades to come the risk of cancer and possibly genetic effects will be great.

The indirect effects of a nuclear explosion will be just as horrendous. Fires could be the worst danger along with infectious diseases in epidemic proportions caused by the destruction of water mains and sewers. Additional long-term effects include changes in the ozone layer, destruction of animal and plant life, alterations of the human gene pool, and serious climactic changes.

The OTA study analyzed several examples of the effects of a single nuclear bomb dropped on modern cities. It calculated that a one-megaton weapon, the equivalent of 1 million tons of conventional explosives, roughly the equivalent of a U.S. Minuteman or a Soviet SS-11, dropped on Detroit would kill 470,000 persons and injure an additional 630,000. The same-size bomb would kill 890,000 residents of Leningrad and injure an additional 1,260,000.

The OTA report summed it up by stating that a nuclear attack involving thousands of warheads "would place in question whether the United States (or the Soviet Union) would ever recover its position as an organized, workable and powerful country."

The 1982 report of the International Independent Commission on Disarmament and Security Issues came to the same conclusion in its statement that "those who optimistically predict a return to ordinary life [after a nuclear attack] within one generation are naive."

The basic facts about the explosive power of the bomb corroborate all of this. An ordinary-size bomb has a warhead with a megaton of power. A megaton is a thousand kilotons. A kiloton is the equivalent of a blast of a thousand tons of concentrated explosives. In the world's arsenals of nuclear weapons there are now 13,000 million tons of TNT. This is the equivalent of 1 million bombs like the one used at Hiroshima. This means that in the world's atomic weapons there is stored the equivalent of 6,000 pounds of TNT for every man, woman, and child in the world.

The United States understood at least dimly in 1946 the global crisis and dilemma that it had brought about by the creation of the nuclear weapon. In the Baruch Plan, offered by the United States in 1946, it was proposed that the American nuclear monopoly be replaced by stages with international control of atomic energy and the bomb. Speaking on June 14, 1946, before the newly created United Nations Atomic Energy Commission Baruch opened his plea with these words: "We are here to make a choice between the quick and the dead . . . if we fail, then we have damned every man to be a slave of fear."

Baruch went on to state that "science has torn from nature a secret so vast in its potentialities that our minds cower from the terror it creates." But, Baruch added, "terror is not enough to inhibit the use of the atomic bomb. The terror created by weapons has never stopped man from employing them.''

Even more prophetically, Baruch noted that ''for each new weapon a defense has been produced in time. But now we face a condition in which adequate defense does not exist.''

Baruch proposed a system of complete control of the entire process of producing atomic weapons, from the mining of the raw materials to the manufacture of new weapons and eventually to the disposal of existing ones. The system was also to apply to the use of nuclear energy for nonmilitary purposes, such as the generation of electric power.

The Baruch Plan was perceived by the Soviets to embody a program by which the United States and the United Nations would control and dominate the development of all forms of nuclear energy and nuclear weapons. To the Soviets this was unacceptable.

History may judge that it was unfortunate that President Truman rejected the advice of his secretary of war, Henry Stimson. A memorandum from Stimson pleaded for direct Soviet-American discussions on the nuclear weapon. In additional documents published for the first time in August 1982, Stimson, who had been secretary of state under Herbert Hoover, warned that Russia would inevitably acquire the bomb and that in the long run humanity would be benefited if the United States entered into a partnership with the Soviet Union and shared with them the secrets of nuclear power. Stimson noted the increasing tensions between the United States and the USSR and went on to note that the relations between these nations ''may be perhaps irretrievably embittered by the way in which we approach the solution of the bomb with Russia.''

Secretary Stimson approached the key question of trust between the United States and the USSR with these words: ''The chief lesson I have learned in a long life is that the only way you can make a man trustworthy is to trust him: and the surest way to make him untrustworthy is to distrust him and show your distrust.''

From the very beginning of the nuclear era the United States demonstrated a distrust for the Soviet Union. There were, of course, many reasons to justify that attitude. Stalin, for example, in a speech on February 9, 1946, took a position with regard to World War II that would be unacceptable to any American government. Stalin said that "the war was the inevitable result of the development of world economic and political forces on the basis of modern monopoly capitalism." Around the same time Stalin furthermore in effect renounced the wartime alliance with the United States and Britain against Hitler's Germany. The origin of the cold war can be traced to Stalin's address in February 1946, which was followed one month later by the famous address of Winston Churchill in Fulton, Missouri, where he charged that an "iron curtain" had descended in Europe.

Complicating the possible acceptance of the Baruch Plan was the fact that the United States rapidly demobilized its armed forces soon after World War II, with the inevitable result that the nuclear weapon was more and more thought to be the chief American deterrent against any attack on Western Europe by the Red Army.

In July 1946 the Soviet government rejected the Baruch Plan. The question remains, however, whether the United States could have done more to renounce or to internationalize its nuclear discovery. Experts on Soviet thinking seem to feel that Joseph Stalin's fear of foreign encirclement and the dark and suspicious perceptions of the Russian people of the outside world made the development of the nuclear weapon by the USSR inevitable. But one cannot help but think that with strong United States and world leadership the bomb first detonated in August 1945 might somehow have been placed into an internationally guaranteed limbo.

The Soviets exploded a nuclear device on August 23, 1949, three years and two months after the Baruch plan had been proposed and years ahead of the date predicted by most American experts. By the time of the initial Soviet test the cold war was a reality. The United States had begun the Marshall Plan and the

Truman administration had adopted George Kennan's policy for the "containment" of the Soviet Union. Five days before the first Soviet test NATO was born. The war in Korea followed soon afterward. West Germany was rearmed and brought into NATO—an event that caused profound consternation in the Soviet Union because that country had been twice invaded by the Germans.

The extensive history of the rise and fall of the Baruch Plan seems to demonstrate that it probably was doomed from the day that it was put forward. But one has to inquire whether or not some form of the Baruch Plan might profitably be developed by the United States and the other nuclear powers. The words of Bernard Baruch, concluding his historic talk on June 14, 1946, quoted these words of Abraham Lincoln: "We shall nobly save, or meanly lose, the last, best hope of earth. The way is plain, peaceful, generous, just—a way which, if followed, the world will forever applaud."

History may judge that the United States made serious mistakes in the way that it approached its proposal of the Baruch Plan. That plan was defeated because the United States came to the conclusion that the Soviet Union is an implacable foe unworthy of a relationship of mutual trust. It was the first time in American history that the United States had come to such a conclusion about an entire nation. That anti-Soviet attitude in effect brought about the nuclear era and has perpetuated that era ever since. If the country had followed the recommendations of Secretary Stimson and made an act of trust in the Soviet Union, would all of history have been changed? That question may seem idle to some, but the ultimate issue in relationships between the United States and the Soviet Union goes back to the words of Stimson that in dealing with any individual "the surest way to make him untrustworthy is to distrust him and show your distrust."

The acquisition of the bomb by Britain in October 1952 was probably inevitable after its development by the two superpowers. But again one has to wonder whether leadership by the

United States or the United Nations might not have provided a European consensus to prevent the emergence of another nation with the nuclear weapon. And again one has to wonder about the failure of President Truman to control the consequences of the movement for which he, more than any other human being, is responsible. History has been kind to Truman's activities during the years 1945 to 1952. But it was precisely during that period that the nuclear madness began and grew. It may be that neither Truman nor most of his contemporaries understood fully the consequences for mankind of the developments they permitted. But surely in any reexamination of recent presidencies this question has to be asked and probed: Could President Truman have prevented, modified, or ameliorated the nuclear curse that now threatens mankind?

France's entry into the nuclear club in 1960 came about for reasons of national pride deepened by the creation of de Gaulle's Fifth Republic in 1958. France may have thought that having the capacity of destroying Soviet cities would relieve France of the burden of participating in another European war. But the ultimate reason was probably France's refusal to accept a status that would be perceived as second class.

Fear of the United States might well have been the major reason why China in 1964, with the aid of weapons-grade uranium from Russia, constructed the atomic weapon. China was probably frightened by America's nuclear threats in the last days of the Korean War, as well as by the debate in the late 1950s in the United States about limited nuclear war. As the Sino-Soviet split developed during the 1960s, China had an added reason to acquire a weapon without which it might not be perceived to be a major power.

India's detonation of a nuclear device in May 1974 was different from the actions of the first four nations that exploded the nuclear bomb. By 1974 the world was aware of the menace that had been created and was pursuing efforts to curb nuclear proliferation. India had to conceal its activities and dissimulate its intentions. India could not say that the acquisition of the nuclear weapon was necessary for its international prestige. Germany, Japan, and other major nations had demonstrated that there were other ways to be in the top rank of countries around the world.

Could the United States or the United Nations have done more during the period from 1945 to 1974 to rid mankind of devices that if used would kill at least 100 million persons? The answer has to be yes. But if it is easy to fault political leaders and international agencies, it is equally easy to fault citizens of the United States and of the world.

The vehemence of the nuclear freeze movement in the early 1980s raises the crucial question as to where the protest and the cries of anguish have been for the past thirty-five years.

Was the conscience of America quieted by some rationalization that the evil intentions of the USSR could justify the retention and the improvement of the bombs that America used at Hiroshima and Nagasaki? Why was there little visible protest against nuclear weapons in the 1950s, the 1960s, and the 1970s? The menace was building up, the bombs were being multiplied by being MIRVed, and the possibility of their first use was becoming more certain and even accepted. But the revulsion and the fear were muted or absent until the early 1980s. This delay in the manifestations of remorse has many causes. But the nuclear freeze movement is generally attributed to the accent by the Reagan administration on the idea of a "winnable" nuclear war and the growing acceptance of the idea by the military that neutron bombs would be used in Europe—at least on a second-strike basis to retaliate against an invasion by conventional Soviet forces.

But the surge of opposition to nuclear weapons in the early 1980s derives from other sources, one of which is the popular understanding, almost for the first time, that a nuclear war is not a war in any traditional sense. Lord Mountbatten put it well just before his death in these words: "The nuclear arms race has no military purpose. Wars cannot be fought with nuclear weapons. Their existence only adds to our perils because of the illusions which they have generated."

The nuclear freeze movement is obviously interested in some concrete, specific plan by which humanity could initiate some rational program to set aside the potential horrors that since 1945 have become a part of mankind's burdens. The nuclear freeze movement is, however, open to the charge that its followers could be seen as persons who think somehow that the threat of nuclear war can be exorcised by shouting repeatedly and even hysterically that the threat exists.

The nuclear freeze movement will be deepened by an understanding of the fact that the United States and the other nuclear powers have not been totally unaware of the unimaginable harm that could result if there is a repetition of Hiroshima and Nagasaki. It is to mankind's efforts at nuclear disarmament that we now turn our attention.

four

Arms Control in the Generation After Hiroshima

The statement in the United Nations charter on disarmament is relatively weak. After World War I the members of the League of Nations required the reduction of national armaments. The situation after World War II, however, was viewed as one requiring that the victorious allies remain strong in order to deter other nations from acting like Germany or Japan. The UN charter, drafted in San Francisco by a group virtually none of whose members knew of the impending nuclear weapon, stressed "collective measures for the prevention and removal of threats to the peace, and for the suppression of acts of aggression. . . ." This approach has not been deemed to have any specific relevance or applicability to the threat of nuclear weapons.

As mentioned already, the Baruch Plan proposed that the manufacture of atomic bombs cease, that existing U.S. bombs should be disposed of, and that the proposed international agency be given possession of all information about the newly discovered weapon. The Soviet Union rejected the Baruch Plan for several reasons. It feared, among other things, that the proposed international ownership and control of atomic facilities would subject the Soviet economy to a body dominated by Western nations united in their desire to hamper communist economic development.

There is apparently no firm consensus on which party or what factors led to the first failure in nuclear arms control by the rejection of the Baruch Plan.

President Truman undoubtedly sensed his great responsibility to history and to humanity. After the Soviet Union had exploded its first nuclear bomb in 1949, President Truman at the UN General Assembly in 1950 indicated a willingness to consider the control of both nuclear and conventional arms. In essence he volunteered to balance nuclear superiority with Soviet conventional-force superiority. But the suggestion came to naught. Actually, President Truman continued to escalate the nuclear arms race. On January 31, 1950, he announced his decision to develop the hydrogen bomb. This was a quantum leap in explosive power. Prior to Truman's decision there was a bitter controversy within the government in which J. Robert Oppenheimer, chairman of the Atomic Energy Commission's General Advisory Committee, expressed opposition to the development of the H-bomb. On the other side was Lewis Strauss, a member and later chairman of the Atomic Energy Commission, who favored the building of the bomb in order to ''stay ahead'' of Soviet nuclear development.

Once again there were those within the scientific and political communities of the United States who wanted to try first for an agreement with the Soviet Union in order to avoid further worsening of relations with the Soviet Union and an elevation of the arms race. The creation of the H-bomb was perhaps the first major event in the action-reaction syndrome between the United States and the USSR that still dominates their relationship with respect to nuclear weapons. In 1950 the Truman administration, without even consulting Congress, began the development of the H-bomb.

One has to conclude that President Truman was the original cold warrior and that his decisions to develop the nuclear weapon, detonate it in Japan, and expand it in the H-bomb set the framework and to some extent controlled the agenda of the entire nuclear era.

General Eisenhower was elected president three days after the first experimental American hydrogen bomb device had been exploded on November 1, 1952. Predictably, the first Soviet H-bomb test came nine months later.

President Eisenhower had an extraordinary sensitivity as to what was transpiring in the arms race during his eight years in the White House. As a general who commanded 12 million men in the most destructive war in human history, he intensely felt his obligation to curb the escalation of nuclear weapons. In the second volume of his memoirs Eisenhower wrote that he often felt that he was struggling with both his own advisors and the Russians. There is no evidence that Eisenhower substantially disagreed with his secretary of state, John Foster Dulles, who enunciated the doctrine that the United States would rely "primarily on the capacity to retaliate, instantly, by means and at places of its own choosing." This doctrine, which came to be known as "massive retaliation," seems inconsistent with many of the things that Eisenhower regularly stated about the cruelty and uselessness of war.

The death of Stalin in 1953 left the Soviet posture on arms control uncertain. In 1954 President Eisenhower, possibly hoping for an opening with the Kremlin, proposed an international limit on the total production of certain strategic materials and a ceiling on military forces. Neither suggestion generated much interest, but the United Nations Subcommittee on Disarmament continued to meet and urge variants of the Baruch Plan. The Soviet Union refused all proposals, fearing that they would permit the United States to have inspection arrangements that would, from the Kremlin's viewpoint, turn into methods of gathering intelligence.

In the almost continuous exchanges on arms control between

the Soviets and the West during the 1950s the fears and anxieties of Moscow are clear. The Soviets kept insisting upon the withdrawal of occupying forces in Germany, the liquidation of overseas U.S. bases, and a sharp reduction in existing levels of military manpower in Europe. The age-old Russian dread of invasion was still acutely present, deepened by the fear that China might depart ideologically from the Soviets—as it did in 1960—and leave the USSR surrounded by actual or potential enemies. The United States, on the other hand, regularly revealed during the 1950s the impact of the cold war in all of its paranoia. It was during the 1950s that millions of Americans came to believe that the communists were preparing to conquer the world covertly or overtly.

In March 1955 President Eisenhower appointed Harold Stassen as his special assistant for disarmament. Stassen, with good intentions but perhaps with some naiveté, urged progressive disarmament steps in Europe. He was, unfortunately, undercut by more cautious spirits at the State Department. In the 1950s the nine-year-old U.S. drive for the elimination of nuclear weapons seemed to wither as the stockpiles increased and the antagonism toward the Soviet empire deepened. President Eisenhower's offer of "open skies"—reciprocal aerial inspection by the United States and the Soviet Union—sounded creative, but it was rejected by the Soviets because it was not a part of a general disarmament program. The Soviet suppression of the Hungarian uprising in 1956 poisoned any climate that might have been favorable to dialogue on arms control.

Enthusiasm for disarmament faded after August 26, 1957, when the Soviet Union announced the first test of an intercontinental ballistic missile (ICBM). Six weeks later on October 4 came the first Sputnik. These two events confirmed every anti-Soviet instinct in the American psyche. President Eisenhower appointed a group of eminent Americans headed by H. Rowan Gaither, Jr., then board chairman of the Ford Foundation. The committee in its report portrayed a rapidly arming Soviet Union with a capability by late 1959 of launching 100 ICBMs against the United States. Although this prediction turned out to be somewhat erroneous, the psychological damage had been done and the projections of Soviet strength formed the basis of the charge of a "missile gap" that Senator John Kennedy used in his 1960 presidential campaign against Eisenhower's vice-president, Richard Nixon.

Perhaps the one lasting and significant development from the 1950s for arms control was the establishment in July 1957 of the International Atomic Energy Agency (IAEA) in Vienna. This initiative resulted from President Eisenhower's "atoms for peace" address in December 1953 to the UN General Assembly, where he proposed that an international agency be established to which all nations would make contributions from their stockpiles of fissionable materials. The agency was created to allocate these nuclear materials for peaceful purposes but to keep them unavailable for military uses. The International Atomic Energy Agency still carries out this worthwhile task, but the agency has no control over materials that the United States and the USSR reserve for their own military purposes. The Soviet Union initially refused to consider the creation of this agency apart from the general issue of arms control. But the Kremlin reversed its position when the United States made it clear that it would proceed with the creation of IAEA with or without Soviet collaboration. The creation of the IAEA illustrates the fact that when the United States takes strong and firm steps on behalf of arms control and when the United States in addition is willing to make some unilateral concessions or sacrifices there is some chance that the Soviets will yield.

In August 1959 another promising development occurred in the formation of the Ten-Nation Disarmament Committee. This committee, with five members from NATO and five from the Warsaw Pact countries, met for several weeks on the question of general and complete disarmament. Whatever promise the new unit might have had faded away when, during a recess from its talks, an American U-2 reconnaissance aircraft was shot down over the Soviet Union. A planned conference between Khrushchev and Eisenhower collapsed. The Ten-Nation Committee on Disarmament was never reconvened. When Francis Gary Powers's U-2 was shot down on May 1, 1960, Khrushchev demanded an apology from Eisenhower, and when this was not forthcoming, he revoked the invitation for Eisenhower to visit the Soviet Union and announced that he would have nothing more to do with the president. The valiant attempts of President Eisenhower to bring about arms control dissolved because of what the Kremlin and Khrushchev deemed to be a deception in the U-2 overflying Russia.

The failure during the 1950s to obtain any resolution of the menace of the nuclear bomb may well be the saddest and most tragic period for arms control. With a highly regarded general in the White House and with both the United States and the USSR still sharing to some extent some of the friendly ties that brought them together during World War II, the 1950s offered opportunities to control nuclear weapons that have never occurred since that time. President Eisenhower's sometimes astonishing statements about the futility of war and the dangers of the industrial-military complex reveal that he saw the arms race getting out of control. Of all American presidents in the nuclear era President Eisenhower may well be the person to have approached the use of force and massive military power with the greatest reluctance and restraint.

What was lacking in Eisenhower's years in the White House was any significant grass-roots drive to bring about a curtailment of nuclear weapons. There was some concern about fallout from testing of nuclear devices. Adlai Stevenson, for example, running in 1956, issued a call for a test ban. The United States government, however, declined to consider a test ban as a separable item in its negotiations with the Soviet Union and continued its testing both in the atmosphere and under the ground.

If the present proponents of some form of nuclear freeze wonder whether their efforts have any lasting effect, they can look back to the 1950s and obtain some sense of assurance that more widespread concern with appropriate political action at that time might well have altered the decisions or nondecisions reached then by the Eisenhower administration and the Congress. The Soviets looked at America during those years and undoubtedly saw a nation united in an almost hysterical fear of communism. Consequently, the Soviets recoiled from making concessions to the United States. If there had been a massive antinuclear movement in America and in Europe during the 1950s, would it have been possible to limit for all time the nuclear bomb to only three nations? Looking back at the period, that hope is not without foundation.

The Congress that saw John Kennedy come to the White House in January 1961 recognized that the United States had no central agency with jurisdiction over arms control or disarmament. The Congress also understood that there is no natural constituency for arms control within the government itself. In September 1961 Congress established the Arms Control and Disarmament Agency (ACDA) with a clear mandate to coordinate all U.S. participation in international negotiations for arms control and disarmament. The director of the ACDA was designated principal advisor to the secretary of state and to the President and, under the direction of the secretary of state, was assigned prime responsibility on all aspects of arms control and disarmament. The Congress, under the leadership of Senator Hubert Humphrey, had the highest aspirations and profound hopes for the ACDA. This new entity was designed to do those creative things that had not been done in the 1950s. It was created to harmonize the almost inherently opposing views of the Pentagon and of the State Department—of the militarists and the diplomats. If the ACDA had lived up to expectations, would it have altered the course of history and brought about some kind of a moratorium in the arms race? It might have. But almost everyone from the beginning—even the Congress that created it—relegated it to a subordinate position within the government. The ACDA was by nature almost a rival rather than ally of the Pentagon, the State Department, and the president. It was designed by the Congress to have the independence and autonomy of agencies such as the Federal Reserve Board. It was also conceived to be like the General Accounting Office—an investigative arm and a watchdog for Congress. It is doubtful, however, whether any agency working on the highly emotional issues involved in nuclear weapons and national security can even approach the role hoped for by the Congress for the ACDA. In the nature of things success in arms control depends almost exclusively upon presidential leadership. Consequently, arms control lagged significantly when President Kennedy was distracted during and after the Cuban crisis, when President Johnson was crippled by his participation in the war in Vietnam, and when President Nixon was weakened by his involvement in Watergate.

An excellent study of the ACDA, *Politics of Arms Control* by Duncan L. Clarke, was published in 1979. It confirms the fact that the role of the ACDA and the future of arms control cannot be determined entirely by a government agency but is ultimately "anchored" in the attitudes of the American people and their elected representatives about arms control, defense expenditures, the Soviet Union, and the role of the United States in world affairs.

Bilateral discussions in 1961 between the United States and the Soviet Union led to the establishment of the Eighteen Nation Disarmament Conference (ENDC). Opening its discussions in Geneva on March 14, 1962, the ENDC eventually concentrated its work on the test-ban negotiations, which were to lead to the acceptance on July 25, 1963, of the limited-test-ban treaty. The progress of the ENDC was diminished, however, by the Cuban missile crisis in October 1962.

The thousand days of the Kennedy administration will be remembered for the inadequate but still spectacular test-ban treaty concluded while Kennedy was in the White House. Pressure to halt atmospheric radioactive pollution reached a crescendo in the late 1950s—especially after the 1954 Bikini explosions carried out by the United States. Fallout from the explosion of a fifteen-megaton hydrogen bomb contaminated a Japanese fishing boat.

Scientists and statesmen all over the world demanded that the United States cease atomic testing. Japanese and German leaders along with the pope appealed to the superpowers. The 1957 session of the UN Disarmament Subcommittee in London could not agree on a test ban, but in 1958 the Soviet Union announced that it was discontinuing testing—pursuant to the announcement by the United States that the United States would cease nuclear testing if the Soviet Union would do likewise. No testing took place from November 7, 1958, until 1961.

After the French conducted their first test in 1960, Khrushchev announced in September 1961 that his country would resume testing and it did. As a result, President Kennedy ordered resumption of underground tests and six months later ordered atmospheric tests.

The Cuban missile crisis probably furnished the key impetus for the 1963 test-ban agreement. On June 10, 1963, President Kennedy in his commencement address at American University stated that the United States would not conduct any further atmospheric tests unless the Soviet Union resumed testing. The address apparently brought about a change in the Soviet position. To the delight of the entire world the Nuclear Test Ban Treaty was signed in Moscow on August 5, 1963. Over one hundred nations have now signed and ratified that document, although France and China have not. France terminated all nuclear tests in the atmosphere in 1974 due to worldwide public opinion; China presumably still tests in the atmosphere.

The treaty was ratified in September 1963 by the United States Senate in a vote of eighty to nineteen.

The Nuclear Test Ban Treaty was, of course, fatally flawed by its failure to ban underground testing. No one can deny the sad fact that it was probably the United States that prevented the adoption of a total ban. There was no agreement among scientists at the time as to the capacity of seismic devices to detect nuclear tests underground. Could they be confused with earthquakes? In December 1962 Khrushchev offered to permit three seismic stations on Soviet soil and allow three on-site inspections per year.

President Kennedy welcomed this uncharacteristic concession but insisted on eight to ten inspections. The Russians withdrew their offer and the two superpowers failed to break the impasse over inspection. As a result the Nuclear Test Ban Treaty prohibited testing in the atmosphere and in the ocean but not under the ground. After the ban, however, both sides lost no opportunities in developing their nuclear weapons, since it turned out that many tests previously carried out above ground could be carried out underground with more reliability. Hence, arms competition was not significantly slowed by the Nuclear Test Ban Treaty, although health hazards from radiation were sharply reduced.

The 1981 volume *Kennedy, Khrushchev, and the Test Ban* by Glenn Seaborg, chairman of the Atomic Energy Commission from 1961 to 1971, relates in detail the heroic struggle that President Kennedy successfully waged for the Nuclear Test Ban Treaty. The pressures by the military and by scientists led by Dr. Edward Teller against the Nuclear Test Ban Treaty were so intense that it may well be that the flawed version ratified by the Senate was possibly the best that could be obtained.

Again the question occurs whether the existence of a massive and politically powerful antinuclear movement in the early 1960s would have brought about a test-ban treaty without the compromise that has allowed the United States and the USSR to continue testing almost as if no ban existed.

Proposals to ban all testing have been advanced since the 1963 treaty. But until the nuclear freeze movement of the early 1980s, these proposals have not aroused broad-based interest or support. In March 1977 President Carter announced his intention to push for a comprehensive test ban. The uncertainty of Senate support and the involvement of the Carter administration with SALT II combined to kill chances that the loopholes in the Nuclear Test Ban Treaty of 1963 could be closed.

Despite the existence of massive testing, there has been little widespread protest against the secret activities that go on to improve the accuracy and enhance the deadliness of weapons even though the whole world knows that neither the improvement nor the enlargement of America's nuclear arsenal can add anything to the security of the nation that the arsenal is designed to protect.

Is the United States culpable for the awful tragedy that occurred in 1963 when the superpowers in effect refused to curtail their ability to make nuclear weapons more hideous? Why did America feel that it should preserve the option of additional testing? Did America think that it would be losing the arms race by capping it? One is reminded of the remark by Jerome Wiesner, President Kennedy's science advisor and president emeritus of MIT, to the effect that the arms race lasting from 1945 to 1963 was a race that Americans were running with themselves.

The world could conclude after the Nuclear Test Ban Treaty of 1963 that the United States was triply responsible—for the creation of the bomb, for its first and only use, and for a decision to pass up the opportunity to take the first steps in banning it by abandoning further testing.

President Reagan was the first chief executive since 1963 to openly reject the possibility of outlawing underground testing. This, of course, was in line with Reagan's consistent approach, since in 1963 he was opposed to the Nuclear Test Ban Treaty in the same way that he opposed the Nuclear Non-Proliferation Treaty in 1968 and both SALT I and SALT II. The Reagan administration in fact sharply increased underground nuclear testing. In the first two years of the Reagan administration funding for testing the nation's nuclear weaponry on 800,000 acres of desert north of Las Vegas increased by 59 percent to $326 million. On August 5, 1982, the eleventh blast of the year occurred at Yucca Flats 2,100 feet under the desert. This nuclear test, the first to be opened to the press in two years, was timed to coincide with the eve of the anniversary of the bombing of Hiroshima on August 6, 1945, and also with the debate on the nuclear freeze in the U.S. House of Representatives. It was the 593rd test announced at the Nevada site since testing began on July 27, 1951.

In July 1982 President Reagan rejected nineteen years of bipartisan American support for a comprehensive nuclear test-ban treaty. It was on July 25, 1963, that American, British, and

Soviet negotiators concluded and initialed in Moscow the Nuclear Test Ban Treaty. President Kennedy said it was a step toward peace—in "a journey of a thousand miles." Since that time every argument emanating from the Pentagon urging the need for additional testing had been rejected by every occupant of the White House. Presidents have also concurred on the advisability of doing what the United States promised to do along with Russia in the Nuclear Test Ban Treaty—pursue a total ban on testing. Two unratified treaties moving toward that goal are the 1974 agreement limiting underground nuclear weapons tests to the equivalent of 150 kilotons of TNT (roughly ten times the Hiroshima bomb) and the 1974 treaty limiting peaceful nuclear test explosions to the same yield.

In 1982 about one-third of the Senate called for ratification of these two treaties. The Reagan White House refused. The reason given was the alleged difficulty in verification—despite the fact that previous administrations found the verification risks acceptable.

The Senate ratified the Nuclear Test Ban Treaty in 1963 by a vote of eighty to nineteen. The nineteen were opposed to any concession of any kind to the Soviets—even if it would bring the United States some benefits. The mentality of those nineteen Senators dominates the Reagan White House and the Pentagon. One can only hope that they will remember and follow the example of the late Everett Dirksen, the Senate Republican leader, who, in switching to support the 1963 treaty said, "I should not like to have written on my tombstone: 'He knew what happened at Hiroshima, but he did not take a first step' "

Kennedy and Khrushchev left the scene soon after the test-ban agreement of 1963. By that time the number and sophistication of ballistic missiles and delivery systems on both sides had risen to unbelievable levels. In the decade from 1945 to 1955 the destructive capacity of nuclear weapons rose by a factor of 1,000. In the decade of 1955 to 1965 the speed of the delivery systems increased in a spectacular manner because of the development of the intercontinental ballistic missile. An ICBM takes thirty minutes to go from the United States to the Soviet Union, whereas a B-52 bomber takes eleven hours. The emergence of the ICBM was almost as revolutionary as the discovery of the nuclear bomb itself. In the 1950s the United States also began the development of submarine-launched ballistic missiles (SLBMs). The concept of carrying multiple warheads on a single missile was refined in the late 1960s with the development of multiple, independently targetable reentry vehicles (MIRVs).

The buildup of weapons on both sides in a short period of time is unbelievable. In fifteen years—1957 to 1972—both superpowers constructed arsenals of a magnitude hitherto unknown in all of human history. The numbers tend to paralyze one's understanding, but the description of the capability of *one* Poseidon submarine shows the staggering power of the new strategic weaponry. The volume *International Arms Control* issued by the Stanford Arms Control Group in 1976 reveals this about one Poseidon: "One such submarine, equipped with 16 MIRV missiles, can deliver warheads to a number of targets greater than the total number of German and Japanese cities subjected to strategic bombing in World War II. For bombers carrying conventional high explosives to deliver a total explosive energy equivalent to that of the nuclear warheads of the missiles of the one submarine would require sorties of several hundred thousand B-52s or more than one million World War II B-17 bombers."

As if this is not totally beyond belief, the Stanford study adds this: "Yet the megatonnage in the missile of that one Poseidon submarine is only a small fraction of one percent of the megatonnage in the U.S. strategic arsenal."

This explosion in offensive systems inevitably led to attempts to build protective or defensive barriers. During the 1950s when strategic nuclear weapons were carried in aircraft, both sides developed highly sophisticated air defense systems. Both superpowers sought to extend the technology developed by anti-aircraft defenses to antiballistic missile (ABM) devices designed to stop incoming strategic warheads. In 1962 the United States after a long series of tests successfully intercepted a missile on a Pacific island fired from an air force base in California. Americans were aware of this development because they had been aroused by reports of an ABM system around Leningrad.

The struggle over the construction of the ABM dominated discussions about arms control in the 1960s. Early in that decade a united Joint Chiefs of Staff recommended a full-scale ABM system. Robert McNamara, secretary of defense from 1961 to 1967, was opposed to the construction of the ABM. He argued that it would not work and that its construction would stimulate the arms race. In a remarkable statement in September 1967, the secretary of defense argued that the ABM would accelerate the arms race: "What is essential to understand is that the Soviet Union and the United States mutually influence one another's strategic plans. Whatever their intentions or our intentions, actions—or even realistically potential actions—on either side relating to the buildup of nuclear forces necessarily trigger reactions on the other side. It is precisely this action-reaction phenomenon that fuels an arms race."

The proposal that the United States construct an elaborate system of antiballistic missile safeguards aroused the American public as no previous controversy on arms control had ever done. The feeling was intense. Demonstrations were widespread. The popular uprising was successful in that President Johnson in February 1967 extended to the Soviets the first offer in U.S. history for talks on the limitation of strategic arms.

The agreements eventually reached in SALT I in 1972 constitute the high point in arms control in the world after Hiroshima and Nagasaki. The superpowers agreed to live in a state of mutual assured destruction. Both sides recognized that they could virtually annihilate the other and that neither could or would build a defense capable of shooting down the incoming missiles of the other. The two parties had different motivations to enter into this startling agreement. The Soviets knew that the United States would go forward with the ABM system if the USSR refused to agree to forgo it. The U.S. leaders knew that a bitter political struggle would occur in Congress and the country over the construction of the ABM. But both parties at least implicitly had to assume before they agreed to SALT I that there was enough rationality operating in the intentions of both parties that neither would detonate nuclear weapons, since this would incite inevitable retaliation with its massive killings and destruction. Both sides, in other words, concluded that neither nation was prepared to enter into an arrangement in which the suicide of the nation must be anticipated.

The freeze in the number of nuclear devices agreed to in SALT I had the advantage of stopping the mad rush of the 1960s. But nothing was done to reverse the awesome totals that had accumulated in an unrestrained and unregulated arms race. Indeed, even worse, the unbelievable accumulation of arms on both sides was accepted and institutionalized.

The ABM treaty, which passed the Senate eighty-eight to two, did not, however, trigger a widespread debate on the morality or the acceptability of living in a state of mutual vulnerability. The debate focused on technical details of the balance in arms arrived at and the prospects for long-range verification. Few observers raised the question that SALT placed the Soviet Union and the West in a situation where both were hostages in that they maintained peace between them only because they were threatened with extinction if they acted otherwise. Throughout history nations have armed against neighbors they perceived as enemies. But never before in human history had nations agreed to be mutually deterred from hostility because they both admittedly had the power on a second-strike basis to practically annihilate the other country.

SALT I did not invent the condition of mutual vulnerability. That was created by the parties during the arms buildup in the 1950s and 1960s. What SALT I did was to give this condition legitimacy and an immunity from challenge. The superpowers agreed to strategic parity—a coexistence in terror or the threat of it—as apparently the only way by which they could coexist at all. Both sides agreed to this condition as the only alternative to a destabilizing and expensive arms race.

SALT I enshrined mutual assured destruction and strategic parity as an essential element of American foreign policy. In the first decade after SALT I it has not generally been deemed relevant or even responsible to question the basic assumptions on which SALT I proceeded. Proposals to cut back on the number of nuclear weapons permitted under SALT I continued to be made, as in the various proposals for SALT II. But few in the mainstream of arms-control thought or strategies seriously proposed a reversal of the fundamental presuppositions of SALT I. The general feeling is that the Soviets have, for the most part, observed SALT and that therefore the United States should stay within the framework of SALT I and seek to improve it.

There are, of course, those who say that the Soviets are engaged in a massive military buildup and that the United States should rescind or modify the commitment it made in SALT I not to build an ABM system. Some would argue that certain plans for the MX missile by implication would violate the ban on the construction of the ABM.

But what the proponents of the nuclear freeze movement are saying, or trying to say, is that they regret the acceptance and validation of mutual assured destruction and they want a rethinking of the very essence of U.S. nuclear strategy as was ratified in SALT I. The proponents of the nuclear freeze may not expressly state their position in these words; indeed, they may simultaneously advocate the ratification of SALT II. But what bothers the freeze proponents most is the pledge and the promise made in SALT I by their nation to the Soviet Union that the United States is prepared to remain unprotected and defenseless against incoming Soviet nuclear missiles but that if they are attacked, they will retaliate against Soviet cities with the inevitable deaths of countless millions of Russian citizens.

SALT I cleared the Senate at a time when the country was deeply involved in the struggle over Vietnam. All of the persons and groups that would have raised the most fundamental moral and ethical questions about the premises of SALT I were engaged in trying to extricate the United States from Southeast Asia. SALT I, moreover, was perceived as a victory for those who were opposed to the United States building elaborate and dubiously effective defenses against incoming missiles.

But during the first decade of SALT I the implications of what the nation did in that treaty became clear to those who paid scant attention to the process leading up to SALT I. These persons were inattentive in part because the terms were arcane, all the options appeared to be equally dismal, and the agreement seemed to be better than the alternative—the inexorable advance of the arms race.

These people—and the whole world—now recognize with horror what America did in SALT I in 1972. In the name of détente and professing to make an act of faith in the sanity and essential humanity of the other side, the United States validated and sanctified in an international agreement its possession of thousands of nuclear weapons. Arms controllers since that time have tried to build on the premises of SALT I by devising methods to prevent a nuclear explosion brought about by mistake or madness. They have worked diligently and ingeniously to invent ways to mitigate the coexistence in terror. But if the framework of SALT I is to remain as the basic architecture between the United States and the USSR, the arms controllers can only continue to explore ways to prevent conflict between two scorpions in a bottle. Those who question the fundamental premises on which SALT I was erected are cast in the role of being unconstructive critics of the best arrangement ever obtained by the superpowers in the nuclear age. Critics of SALT I are dismissed as naive believers in unilateral disarmament who are unable or unwilling to admit that nuclear weapons are the burden of mankind forever.

The harsh reality is that those who want to return to the situation prior to SALT I have a hard time becoming a part of the debate. These critics of SALT I reject the morality or the decency of using the threat of savage amounts of force to deter a country whose motives the United States suspects or distrusts. But those who are opposed to SALT I are like those persons who say that crime will continue despite all kinds of draconian penalties until those who are suspected of being prone to crime are persuaded not by force but by logic and love not to attempt crime. Those who worry about the impact and implications of SALT I are, in other words, not decrying the art and science of arms control but pleading that the United States enter into an entirely new series of processes intended to mitigate and even to eliminate the perceived hostility of the USSR toward the West.

Proponents of additional methods of arms control behold a world ten years after SALT I that has become inured to the possibility of killings so numerous as to be unimaginable. Furthermore, those who wonder about the wisdom of SALT I know that it cannot effectively reach new weapons such as the Cruise missile, which is easily concealed, hard to detect or count, and which can do all of the damage that an ordinary nuclear weapon can do. Similarly, SALT I does not offer verifiable protection against missiles launched from outer space by satellite technology—a development that appears to be more and more possible.

But the fundamental problem with SALT I is its assumption that the antagonism and enmity of the USSR toward the United States and the West is so profound and permanent that the United States must erect against this nation machinery for a retaliatory strike so immense that its very presence is adequate and necessary to deter the Soviets from doing that which they otherwise would be prone to do.

The level of hostility and hate that this assumes to be an unalterable part of Soviet intentions is very high. Americans who want to be good neighbors and even friends with all of the nations of the world find this assumption of hostility and hate very troubling. They have to surmise that if the hostility and hatred do exist at levels assumed by SALT I, then it follows that the Soviets perceive or misperceive the United States to have comparably deep hostile intentions toward the USSR. The obvious question is: Is it not possible somehow by some means to extend détente, to encourage dialogue, to deepen the basic feelings that all human beings have for other human beings, so that two vast nations do not have to live at sword point, armed against each other as if both were savage adversaries restrained only by the certainty that aggression is the same as suicide?

five

Carter and Salt II: Reagan and START

At his first formal press conference President Carter stressed his desire to reach an agreement on SALT II. He approved of the formulas agreed to by President Ford at Vladivostok, adding that he also would set aside until SALT III the disputed issues about the Soviet Backfire and the U.S. Cruise missiles. A few days earlier Brezhnev had expressed the desire of his government for a strategic-arms-limitation agreement. The fact that certain agreements in SALT I were due to expire in October 1977 gave reason to both sides to resume talks promptly.

In March 1977 President Carter, in a demonstration of his desire for arms control, sent Secretary of State Cyrus Vance to Moscow with an eleven-point comprehensive plan for arms control and arms reduction. In his 1979 book *The SALT Experience*, Thomas W. Wolfe states that "this comprehensive package amounted to a radically innovative proposal." In Wolfe's judgment the proposal would "for the first time in the history of SALT" make "a real cut into the strategic 'muscle' of both sides." The Carter package was designed to restrict the modernization process and thereby to place curbs on the further growth of Soviet counterforce capabilities. These curbs would, of course, also cut against the United States in its efforts to enlarge its nuclear armada.

The brusque rejection by the Kremlin on March 28, 1977, of the Carter proposals suggested that the Soviets were driven by deep fears that the United States wanted to deprive them of their security and even their status as a superpower. On March 31 Gromyko charged that the proposals were "aimed at obtaining unilateral advantages for the United States, to the detriment of the Soviet Union." He detailed Soviet grievances on several points, indicating his displeasure at what he perceived to be the continued inequality for the Soviets of the American forward-based nuclear bombers being excluded from the negotiations.

The real reasons for the rejection of the package are not entirely clear. Speculation continues on the possibility of extrinsic reasons for the Soviet rejection of the most drastic plan ever put forward for arms control by either of the parties to SALT. Was it Soviet annoyance over President Carter's highly visible accent on human rights in the USSR? Was it the preannouncement to the press of the plan by the Carter administration before Vance even left for Moscow? Was it the presence of Zbigniew Brzezinski in the Carter administration that the Soviets feared—an émigré from Eastern Europe with all of the characteristically anti-Soviet attitudes of that class? Or was it, as the opponents of SALT would insist, one more reason to demonstrate the soundness of the proposition that the leaders of the Soviet Union want to conquer the world and want to do it with the least possible disruption or inconvenience to the citizens of the Soviet Union?

Those who for many years had been urging that arms control and disarmament be brought about by the superpowers were saddened and shaken by the rejection of Carter's creative proposals. Those who were inclined to feel that SALT I only institutionalized and validated the coexistence in terror were also disappointed because apparently no improvement in that process seemed to be possible.

Despite the strong rejection of Carter's proposals in March 1977, the Soviet leadership later that year resumed negotiations for SALT II. The negotiations were difficult, but SALT II was eventually signed in Vienna on June 18, 1979, by Presidents Carter and Brezhnev.

Even for experts some of the provisions of the fifty-page SALT II agreement are arcane and bewildering. For the nonexpert, SALT II can be a puzzle, a riddle, a muddle. A careful reading of the excellent study of the story of SALT II in *Endgame* by Strobe Talbott can leave one still undecided as to whether SALT II is a desirable development of the best features of SALT I or whether it is a porous agreement that the parties can manage to evade if they so desire.

The complexity of the language and the almost incomprehensibility of the concepts in SALT II left even the best informed without very strong feelings about SALT II. It was hard to think that disarmament was around the corner when the Soviet Backfire medium-range bomber was excluded from the total aggregate of allowable strategic weapons. It was not particularly reassuring to have a commitment from the Soviets that they would not build into this plane the capability of striking targets within the United States. Nor did SALT II look like a bold strike for arms control by the United States government when it insisted that the U.S. Cruise missiles should not be included in the ceilings of SALT II. These devices, Cruise missiles, are unmanned, self-propelled guided missiles that can be launched from aircraft, submarines, surface ships, and ground platforms. The United States retained the right to use these in return for permission for the Soviets to use their Backfire bombers.

SALT II does, however, bring about real progress in arms control. It would require the Soviet Union to dispose of more than 250 of their missiles or bombers. In addition, the subceiling on MIRVed ICBMs would oblige the Russians to dismantle about 10 percent of their most threatening weapons. The agreement, moreover, provides for an overall ceiling of 2,250 strategic nuclear launchers, a subceiling of 1,320 launchers with multiple warheads, and a further subceiling of 1,200 for launchers of MIRVed land-based missiles and submarine-based missiles. Most importantly, SALT II contains a prohibition on the testing and deployment of all but one new ICBM in the lifetime of the agreement.

SALT II continues the operation of the Standing Consultative Commission, established in SALT I, to provide assurance of compliance with treaty obligations and to be a sort of forum and clearing house for the parties in their quest to enhance strategic stability.

The negotiators for the United States in the SALT II deliberations had to be continuously careful not to grant concessions that would induce thirty-four United States senators to defeat the treaty. Negotiators also had to be very mindful of America's commitments to NATO. Europe would not look kindly on a treaty that weakened or even questioned America's pledge to be prepared with nuclear weapons in Europe in the event of the presence or the threat of an overwhelming attack by conventional forces or an actual attack by nuclear weapons.

Judgments on the advisability and usefulness of SALT II will continue to be mixed. There is reason for great skepticism over the efficacy both of SALT I and SALT II because of their exclusion of all nonstrategic weapons. The exclusion of tactical or theater weapons is not really logical, since their characterization as nonstrategic does not do away with the fact that when detonated they produce the same catastrophic results as strategic bombs. A perceptive English author with vast experience in nuclear strategy, Solly Zuckerman, states in his 1982 book *Nuclear Illusion and Reality* that negotiations on nuclear arms should include *all* nuclear weapons and hence the acronym should not be SALT but NALT—Nuclear Arms Limitation Talks.

Pax Christi, an international Catholic peace movement with headquarters in Belgium, speaking through its affiliate in the United States, came out against SALT II. This group, whose members need not be pacifists, dates from the beginning of the nuclear age and is committed to the centrality of Christian nonviolence. In the view of Pax Christi, SALT II legitimated the existing American arsenal—a destructive power of 615,000 Hiroshima bombs. Ironically, Pax Christi was joined in its opposition to the ratification of SALT II by the Committee on the Present Danger—a group that opposed SALT II not because it did too little but because it gave away too much. Catholic Bishop Thomas J. Gumbleton of Detroit argued the case for Pax Christi in *Commonweal* magazine on March 2, 1979. He asserted that an approval of the placing of a ''cap'' on nuclear weapons as SALT II did would be comparable to supporting a ''cap'' on the number of torture chambers permitted to governments. SALT II, moreover, the bishop wrote, will not reduce or reverse the arms race and is not ''a first step out of an evil situation.'' Bishop Gumbleton agreed with Karl Barth, a leader in the German churches' resistance to Hitler, that the most vital issue facing Christianity is its inability to take a definite stand against nuclear weapons. Accordingly, the bishop felt that the role of religious leaders is not to endorse SALT II and work for its ratification but to educate the world to understand in the words of the Second Vatican Council, that ''the arms race in itself is an act of aggression against the poor.''

Arguing in the same issue of *Commonweal* on behalf of SALT II, Father J. Bryan Hehir, associate secretary of the Office of International Justice and Peace of the United States Catholic Conference, pointed out that SALT II lowers the permissible number of strategic nuclear delivery vehicles from 2,400 to 2,250, which is the first reduction of offensive weapons in the history of the nuclear arms race. He also pointed out that although the actual reduction is marginal, the superpowers did agree in SALT II that they would limit themselves to produce and deploy only one new missile during the life of the treaty. Father Hehir also worried about what would happen to the arms spiral if SALT II were rejected. Recognizing that the arms race is ''generated by a quasi-independent technological dynamic,'' he looks to SALT II as a chance ''to impose political control. . . .'' Conceding that the middle ground that he staked out between the clarity of the Pax Christi position and the certainty of the position of the Committee on the Present Danger may appear to be a compromise, Father Hehir identified it as a position that "supports what is presently possible in pursuit of a larger vision of what must be made possible."

It is not clear whether SALT II will ever be a live option again for the Congress or the country. It is, nonetheless, still the most comprehensive and sophisticated development in arms control in the nuclear era.

History may judge that President Carter made a mistake when he withdrew his support for SALT II after the invasion of Afghanistan. Carter may have sensed that he would not get the necessary two-thirds vote in the Senate, or he may have dropped SALT II in order to appear aggressively anticommunist in the 1980 campaign. What is clear is that Carter's abandonment of SALT II may have been the death knell of the entire SALT process for a long time to come. The irony is, however, that the Reagan administration is continuing to observe all of the guarantees made in the unratified SALT II agreement. This anomaly prompted former Secretary of State Henry Kissinger, who had testified in favor of SALT II, to remark that "I have a great difficulty understanding why it is safe to adhere to a nonratified agreement while it is unsafe formally to ratify what one is already observing."

In any event, the persistent position of the Reagan administration that SALT II is "fatally flawed" will dominate the discussion on arms control for the foreseeable future. It is this impasse that helped to bring forth the nuclear freeze movement. The "freezeniks" do not necessarily reject the SALT process as fruitless, but they are desperate for some new initiative, some way by which the nuclear stockpiles can be cut back and the global dangers diminished. In 1982 the nuclear freeze movement was unfocused and not fixed to any specific political objectives. There are many reasons to suggest that the ratification of SALT II is still the most desirable of all of the options available to the nuclear freeze movement. But even the most ardent advocates of the SALT process must concede that perhaps one of the best features of SALT II is that it gets the superpowers to SALT III.

It is a sign of the intractability of issues involved in arms control that President Carter, more sensitive and articulate about the nuclear menace than any president in the nuclear era, was able to accomplish so little in his four years in the White House. It is also a sign of the volatility and the inscrutability of the issues that SALT II was not defeated on its merits or demerits but by extrinsic factors such as the Soviet brigade in Cuba, American hostages in Iran, and the Soviet invasion of Afghanistan.

During the first fifteen months of the Reagan administration—for the first time in ten years—there were no negotiations at all with the Soviet Union on nuclear weapons. The Reagan approach to the problem differed radically from at least his three immediate predecessors. On August 20, 1980, candidate Reagan stated that "Our nuclear deterrent forces must be made survivable as rapidly as possible to close the window of vulnerability before it opens any wider." Although several billion dollars were added to the military budget in 1981 and 1982, President Reagan on March 31, 1982, reaffirmed the alleged existence of the window of vulnerability, stating that "the Soviet Union does have a definite margin of superiority."

Reagan's hostility to SALT II was made clear by his appointment of Eugene Rostow to head the Arms Control and Disarmament Agency. Rostow was a founding member and former chairman of the Committee on the Present Danger, one of the leading groups in the fight against SALT II. Rostow's article, "The Case Against SALT II," in *Commentary* magazine for February 1979, claimed that SALT II would condemn the United States to strategic inferiority.

It was Reagan's silence about arms control during 1981 that was one of the major forces for the birth of the nuclear freeze movement. Former President Carter noted this in his first address with open criticism of Reagan on December 17, 1981, where he stated that in the antinuclear demonstrations in Europe, "Most of the hundreds of thousands are demonstrating against us and not against the much more culpable leader of the Warsaw Pact."

In the same address Carter, recounting the "extended bipartisan effort" on behalf of SALT I and SALT II, praised the process and lamented that "now we have seen a radical American departure from this long-standing policy." Lashing out at Reagan and reminding him that SALT I, which has lapsed, and SALT II, which was not ratified, do not have the force of law, Carter asked, "What modifications to the existing treaties would make them acceptable to the Administration?"

The sponsorship of the nuclear freeze resolution by Senators Kennedy and Hatfield, the massive demonstration for the freeze in New York City on June 12, 1982, and the pleas of the NATO nations for action finally led to the Reagan address on arms control at Eureka College on May 8, 1982. Renaming SALT START, the president proposed cutting ballistic missile warheads from roughly 7,500 for each side to 5,000—of which no more than half, or 2,500 could be on land-based missiles. The United States, with only 2,152 land-based warheads, fits easily under that ceiling and could even increase the number up to 2,500. The Soviet Union, on the other hand, with about 72 percent of its warheads based on land, would have to scale back by some 3,000 warheads what it considers to be the centerpiece of its defense.

Again the Reagan plan would limit the number of land-based and sea-based missiles to a total of 850 on each side. To reach that level the Soviets would have to give up 1,550 launchers and the United States 850.

There are other measures proposed in START that are one-sided—such as the accent on total weight rather than accuracy and sophistication—a proposal that puts the Soviets at a serious disadvantage.

While arms controllers and advocates of a nuclear freeze are glad that the Reagan administration has not allowed the SALT process to collapse completely, there are many who feel that the Reagan administration at Geneva is offering proposals that cannot be accepted by the Soviets and that they are being offered as a way of stonewalling and buying time while the administration builds the MX, Minuteman III, and Trident II missiles. The construction of these and other weapons will close the supposed window of vulnerability by making America's land-based missiles invulnerable. In going forward with these plans the Reagan administration may violate SALT I. If the so-called dense-pack scheme of basing the MX is chosen, there may be a violation of the 1972 ABM treaty. If the "dense-pack" is developed, it will mean the first repudiation by the U.S. government of any of the commitments made by the United States in SALT I and SALT II.

START does not deal with what is perhaps the most destabilizing of all new weapons—the new form of the U.S. Cruise missile. In 1982 the Pentagon was preparing to deploy over three thousand of these nuclear-armed missiles on B-52 and B-1 bombers—about five hundred on the ground in Europe and many more aboard submarines. To be sure, they are not "strategic" weapons, but the proliferation of these highly accurate and difficult-to-verify devices is surely a cause of great concern to the Soviets.

START in Geneva is different from all previous discussions in the SALT process in that in all prior talks the parties had assumed that a rough parity existed. The Reagan administration, convinced that the USSR has a margin of superiority, appears to regard the construction of Trident II, the MX, the B-1, and the Stealth bomber as nonnegotiable.

If the START talks fail, the result would be "almost a doubling of strategic weapons within a decade," according to the former chairman of the Joint Chiefs of Staff, General David C. Jones. If the START talks stop or stumble, the nuclear freeze movement would probably grow beyond anything comparable ever witnessed in the nuclear age. The advocates of the freeze would feel that the last hope for any rational restraint on the arms race had collapsed.

The future of START depends less on the intrinsic value to the parties of the bargaining chips they have to offer than on the state of the economy in the superpowers and the status of public opinion. If the antinuclear movement is strong and bids fair to be a significant factor in the election of 1984, the START talks might suddenly yield some startling results. If, on the other hand, the fear of a Soviet military buildup grips the American people, the START talks could practically end the entire SALT process.

It is clear that arms control is at a crossroads in 1983. Many profound factors are operating. There is a latent anxiety among Americans that surfaces when they realize that it has been their nation that has escalated the arms race. It was America that invented the A-bomb, the H-bomb, MIRVs, and Cruise missiles. At the same time Americans tend to retreat from their antinuclear feelings when they hear some of the worst-case scenarios of the Pentagon strategists. What would Americans do, for example, if the Soviet Union somehow managed to knock out all of America's land-based ICBMs and immediately on the hot line demanded the surrender of the United States to the Kremlin? If the United States did not surrender, the scenario postulates, its major cities would be destroyed before America could retaliate by striking back on Russian missiles or its cities. Unless one is prepared to brush aside completely scenarios of this kind as impossible, they give pause to even the most adamant opponent of nuclear weapons.

Confronted and confounded by miserable options on all sides and intimidated by the nuclear experts with their esoteric vocabulary and their scientific elitism, Americans are at a loss as to how to relieve themselves of their anxiety concerning the nuclear holocaust that more and more people are predicting is inevitable. In the early 1980s a nuclear freeze was attractive because it sounded plausible. At least it was a way of giving credence to the certainty that in nuclear arms control little has happened except as a result of a broad-based popular protest. In the late 1950s and the early 1960s there was public concern over radioactive fallout from the atmosphere that helped President Kennedy in 1963 to negotiate the Nuclear Test Ban Treaty with the Soviet Union: women's groups demonstrated outside the White House because of the possibility of strontium 90 in children's milk. In the late 1960s and early 1970s it was public opposition to the Sentinel and Safeguard antiballistic systems that induced President Nixon to negotiate the ABM Treaty. And in 1980 and 1981 it was the opposition of farmers and ranchers as well as the Mormon church in Utah and Nevada that made it impossible to carry out President Carter's plan to dig up thousands of square miles to build the MX.

But the nuclear freeze, despite the wide support it enjoys—as revealed in every public opinion poll—fails to get anything close to majority support if people think that the freeze will make the United States inferior to the Soviet Union. People might not be able to define very precisely superiority or parity or equivalency, but they feel deep down that the United States is in a race against an adversary that will attack the United States as soon as there is the appearance of any sign of weakness in America's military posture. The cold war mentality, in other words, is endemic and seemingly ineradicable in the American mind. This attitude was described in *Commentary* in February 1979 by Eugene Rostow, then the Sterling professor of law at Yale, who wrote that the Soviet Union since the late 1950s had been engaged in a massive military buildup "designed to revise the relationship which determined the outcome of the Berlin airlift, the Korean War and the Cuban missile crisis."

There are, of course, many reasons to suppose that the USSR would like to do to Europe and to the United States what it has done through the years to Hungary, Czechoslovakia, Afghanistan, and Poland. But to translate the fears that America has had of Russia for almost forty years into the feeling that the Soviets would use nuclear weapons to carry out their expansionist ambitions is imputing to them an irrationality and an inhumanity that distorts all of reality. It assumes or asserts that the Soviets are so possessed of ambition and lust for world conquest that they will take any risk to themselves and commit any series of heinous crimes if by so doing they will accomplish their objectives. This picture of the Soviets is very close to that which

President Reagan gave in his address in June 1982 to the Special Session on Disarmament of the United Nations General Assembly. It is an image of the Soviet Union that has been a part of the American psyche for almost two generations and that will be very hard to alter or transform. But what it misses or seeks to avoid is the unique nature of the predicament in which both the Soviet Union and the United States find themselves. The Soviets simply have to know and realize that if they want to achieve world conquest by nuclear weapons, they will in all probability achieve this by the obliteration of the 127 Russian cities that the United States has targeted for attack by nuclear missiles.

Could any leader or any bureaucracy in the Kremlin really seriously consider such an option? Is there anything in Marxism or Soviet imperialism that would prompt people even to think of such a scenario? Apparently there are Pentagon planners who think there is. At least they say that their job is to protect the lives of 230 million Americans and their allies in the NATO nations from every conceivable nuclear attack, however improbable or bizarre. And that is the state of mind that deep down the majority of Americans have accepted. They recognize that the United States has assumed certain dangers in preparing itself to prevent in every conceivable way a first strike by the Soviets. But whatever dangers America might encounter as a result of its possession of 30,000 nuclear weapons, the American people have apparently found them acceptable and indeed necessary for the protection of America's military security and its national interests.

It is that mentality to which candidate Reagan appealed and that he exploited when he proclaimed that America has to be rearmed. It is that feeling that induced the Congress to vote vast new sums for the 1983 military budget. And it will be that pro-found—is it pathological?—dread of the Soviets that is the ulti-mate reason why the United States in 1983 is spending $133 billion on NATO and maintains 337,000 American military per-sonnel. More billions will undoubtedly be spent during the 1980s in Southwest Asia, the Persian Gulf, and Central America to combat what is perceived as an ongoing Soviet geopolitical movement for world conquest.

The architects of the nuclear freeze movement have to try to fashion political objectives that will not collide head-on with all of the fears and phobias that Americans have about Soviet intentions. But these objectives have to be tangible and realizable. In a movement that involves so much metaphysical speculation about the Soviets' view of reality it is almost inevitable that there will be—perhaps for a long time—ambiguities, uncertainties, lurchings, even eclipses of the movement itself. All of the near-frenzied activity in the early 1980s of scientists, physicians, lawyers, and clergy on behalf of nuclear disarmament may flounder if the American people will not yield in their present determination to protect their country from every conceivable nuclear attack regardless of the cost to the American taxpayer. America's hostile obsession with communism may make it blind to the danger to the American people and its allies from a nuclear weapon being detonated by a human or computer mistake or by the action of a terrorist or a madman. If that attitude abides—and it is clearly the position of the Reagan administration—the nuclear freeze movement will have to go to the very heart of the issue and probe deeply into the American psyche to try to find out why it is impossible to convince Americans that the Soviets, however wrongful some of their deeds may have been, are people like ourselves who love their children, who dislike genocide as much as we do, and who do not want to be the gangsters or outlaws of international society that Americans have asserted them to be during most of the nuclear era.

Clearly, the nuclear freeze movement does not want to tackle the task of reversing something very profound in the American consciousness. It would be easier to talk about the revival of SALT, the extension of START, the opening of new talks with the USSR, and the improvement of means of verification. But these are not the ultimate problems and, as the melancholy history of arms-control demonstrates, improvements in those areas can coexist with a simultaneous escalation in the level of calculated and threatened violence.

America has some awesome questions to answer. Does it want to protect "the free world" from the "menace" of communism even if the price for doing so is the death of 200 million persons or more, the contamination of the earth's environment for centuries to come, and even the destruction of one-half or more of the people of the United States? Although the logical answer has to be no, the reply is clouded by the almost omnipresent fear of many Americans that the United States would somehow be lost if it should become number two to the Soviet Union.

Another question that Americans must answer is "linkage." If the Soviet Union engages in adventurist activities as it did in Ethiopia and Angola, should the United States "punish" it by slowing down the negotiations on arms control? In the past "linkage" has interfered hardly at all in the SALT process. President Nixon was bombing North Vietnam as the SALT I talks neared completion in 1972 and they were not interrupted. Détente was confronting daunting difficulties in 1979, but President Carter signed SALT II. Those who want to postpone arms talks until Soviet behavior has improved operate from the false premise that the United States is granting favors to Russia by engaging in arms-control negotiations. The fact is that arms talks can benefit the United States as much as the other side. The Reagan administration in its negotiations in Geneva may well seek to use "linkage," since this will give the Reagan administration an opportunity to do those things that they conceive to be necessary to overcome the alleged superiority of the USSR.

In 1983 the arms-control community is as gloomy and pessimistic as it has ever been since it emerged in the early 1960s. The architects of the nuclear test ban and the framers and technicians of SALT I and SALT II are fearful as never before. Some of them have become advisors to the nuclear freeze movement and hope that they are in the process of making it the most promising messenger of hope to a world stricken with fear of a nuclear holocaust.

six

Congress and the Nuclear Freeze in 1982

On August 5, 1982, the United States House of Representatives spent nine hours of deliberations and debate on the nuclear freeze. The allotment of time was in itself unusual, even extraordinary. The measure before the House was not a law but only a joint resolution; it was furthermore a proposal doomed to failure since the Senate Foreign Relations Committee had already rejected it. It was clearly the broad-based, grass-roots nuclear freeze movement that impelled the Foreign Affairs Committee of the House of Representatives to report out House Joint Resolution 521 mandating a nuclear weapons freeze. The vote on a bipartisan basis was impressive—twenty-eight to eight.

The momentum for some congressional action on the nuclear freeze seemed overwhelming. The final vote of rejection by the House of 204 to 202 was surprising and disappointing to the proponents of the freeze. It is not surprising, however, if one looks at the long resistance to arms control by the Congress and the country—a resistance that is particularly pronounced in the Reagan administration.

The House of Representatives in its historic debate on the nuclear freeze on August 5, 1982, was reacting almost in desperation to the repeated rejections by the Reagan administration of negotiations and agreements related to America's international responsibilities. The Reagan White House had walked away from the long-negotiated Law of the Sea, had declined to ratify the threshold test ban and peaceful nuclear explosion, had rejected two fishing treaties with Canada, and, of course, had repudiated SALT II.

House Joint Resolution 521 was supported by all of the civic, religious, and antinuclear groups in the nation. Cosponsored before the debate on August 5 by 183 members of the House, it had the endorsement of many labor unions, Common Cause, the National Educational Association, the U.S. Conference of Mayors, and the Democratic leadership of the House. Its failure therefore was a stunning blow and a reversal that left the nuclear freeze movement in a quandary as to its next step. The only consolation for those who endorsed the freeze was the fact that every member of Congress who voted against the joint resolution could be portrayed as the single individual who prevented passage of a measure that at least would have been a signal to the administration that the Congress finally was prepared to reverse its decades-old supine attitude toward the arms race.

The hearings and the report on the House Measure (No. 97-640) make reference to the fact that nuclear freeze resolutions had been endorsed by 125 city councils around the nation, by one or both houses in twelve state legislatures, and by nearly four hundred New England town meetings. The fact that the freeze proposal was on the ballots in ten states—including New York, Pennsylvania, California, Michigan, and New Jersey— added to the political motivation to bring the measure to the floor. Even the fact that the Reagan administration began START talks in Geneva on June 29, 1982, did not deter the leaders of the House from bringing to the floor a proposal that under almost any interpretation would be perceived to be a "lecture" by the House to the administration as to how to conduct its nuclear negotiations. The White House, the State Department, and the Pentagon recognized this and, in an extraordinary display of concentrated lobbying, defeated the nuclear freeze proposal. Whether the administration succeeded in diffusing the entire nuclear freeze movement remains to be seen. But it is clear that on August 5, 1982, the day before the thirty-seventh anniversary of Hiroshima, the freeze movement received a blow that may either be its death knell or its second spring.

The nuclear freeze resolution called for a mutual and verifiable halt to the testing, production, and further deployment of nuclear warheads, missiles, and other delivery systems. It also called for prompt approval of SALT II "provided accurate verification capabilities are maintained." A report on House Joint Resolution 521 stressed the commitment of the Reagan administration to abide by the provisions of SALT II, predicted that the START talks would not lead to any easy or quick negotiations, and that the United States would be therefore wise to formalize "agreements already adhered to by both sides"—especially "in light of an imminent Soviet leadership succession."

In one version of the freeze proposal the measure urged that SALT II be submitted to the Congress as an executive agreement; an executive agreement becomes law by a majority vote of both houses and, unlike a treaty, does not require a two-thirds vote in the Senate.

On first inspection the nuclear freeze resolution appears to be a bland affirmation of all those things that persons and groups, terrified of nuclear weapons, have been saying for years. The preamble to the resolution states that "the greatest challenge facing the earth is to prevent the occurrence of nuclear war by accident or design." The resolution continues by lamenting that "the increasing stockpiles of nuclear weapons and nuclear delivery systems by both the United States and the Soviet Union have not strengthened international peace and security but in fact enhanced the prospect for mutual destruction."

But a study of the nuclear freeze resolution demonstrates that it is in effect a frontal attack on the basic premises and assumptions of the approach of the Reagan administration to the Soviets. The resolution takes a position on the state of strategic balance between the superpowers diametrically opposed to that of the Reagan White House. The freeze resolution is grounded on the assumption that there is now a rough parity in the nuclear forces of the United States and the USSR, that that parity was recognized when both signed SALT II, and that now is the moment in which both sides can "freeze" all of their nuclear activities.

For authority for this conclusion the advocates of the freeze pointed to an article "Russian and American Capabilities" in the *Atlantic Monthly* for July 1982 by Jerome Wiesner, arms control advisor to President Kennedy and president emeritus of MIT. Dr. Wiesner states categorically that "at the moment neither the United States nor the Soviet Union has a meaningful strategic advantage. A window of vulnerability does not exist." As a result, Wiesner concludes: "The most obvious and sensible step for the United States at the moment is to add nothing to our nuclear forces, and to seize this opportunity to press for a freeze on the development, testing and deployment of all nuclear weapons and new delivery systems by each side." Wiesner warns that "if this opportunity for arms control is not taken the job will only grow more difficult in the future. The weapons of today are easy to count and monitor, but those of tomorrow won't be. The cruise missile, the satellite bomber, and far more accurate guidance systems would lead to a nightmare world. . . ."

To those who believe in the existence of the "window of vulnerability" the bedrock assumptions of the freeze advocates are falsehoods and fantasies. The critics of the freeze arrive at their position by inspecting the total holdings of strategic nuclear weapons by both sides as in the following chart taken from U.S. government unclassified sources as of mid-1982. The chart compares the number of missiles and warheads in land-based ICBMs, submarine-missiles, and in the strategic bomber forces of the United States and the Soviet Union.

STRATEGIC NUCLEAR FORCES					
UNITED STATES		WARHEADS PER MISSILE	USSR		WARHEADS PER MISSILE
LAND-BASED INTER-CONTINENTAL-	TITAN II 53 MINUTE-MAN II 450	1 1	SS-II 580 SS-13 60 SS-17 150 SS-18 308 SS-19 300		1 1 4 up to 10 6
RANGE BALLIS-TIC MISSILE LAUNCHERS (ICBMs)	MINUTE-MAN III 550	3			
TOTAL ICBMs	1.053		1.398		
TOTAL ICBM WARHEADS	2.100 approx.		6.000 approx.		
SUBMARINE-BASED* BALLISTIC MISSILES (SLBMs)	POSEIDON 320 TRIDENT I 224	10 8	GOLF & HOTEL 30 SS-N-6 396 SS-N-8 & 18 504 TYPHOON 20		1 1–2 1–3
TOTAL SLBMs	544		950		
TOTAL SLBM WARHEADS	5.000 approx.		1.500 approx.		
BOMBERS	B-52 347 FB-111 63		BEAR 100 BISON 45 BACKFIRE 200		
TOTAL BOMBERS†	410		345		
TOTAL MISSILES	1.597		2.348		
TOTAL MISSILE WARHEADS	7.100		7.500		
TOTAL MISSILES & BOMBERS	2.007		2.693		

* Includes on the U.S. side: 20 Poseidon submarines with 320 Poseidon missiles, 11 Poseidon submarines with 176 Trident I Missiles, and 2 Trident submarines with 48 Trident I missiles.
Includes on the Soviet side: 1 Golf- and 7 Hotel-class submarines, 25 Yankee-class submarines with 396 missiles, 36 Delta-class submarines with 504 missiles, and 1 Typhoon submarine with 20 missiles

† Chart does not include number of bombs carried on bombers or more than 3,000 air-launched cruise missiles to be deployed on U.S. bombers. Also not shown are several hundred cruise missiles to be deployed on U.S. submarines.

On the basis of the figures in the chart above and on other evidence, the Reagan administration contends that over the past ten years the Soviets have achieved a definite margin of superiority, while the United States has not improved its strategic nuclear forces during that period. The argument is that the Soviet advantage in ICBMs (6,000 to 2,100 as recorded on the chart) gives them the capability of destroying 90 percent of the ICBM forces of the United States. According to this scenario the United States would have to launch submarine-based missiles in a retaliatory strike. Since these lack the accuracy or the explosive power to destroy land-based missile silos, the United States would be left with the options of either destroying Soviet cities, recognizing that the Soviets could respond with a second strike, or bowing to a political accommodation with Moscow.

The House Committee Report on the nuclear freeze resolution states that this scenario "is divorced from reality." The Soviets would need 2,000 perfectly coordinated warheads to destroy America's 1,052 ICBMs in their silos; all of the 2,000 would have to be perfectly synchronized in order to avoid mutual destruction by the phenomenon called "fratricide," which "can cause the nuclear explosives of some warheads to affect other warheads before detonation." Even if, moreover, Soviet missiles were somehow able to knock out the 24 percent of America's nuclear weapons that are its ICBM force, the other side would be struck with retaliatory weapons that are "on station in invulnerable submarines"—not to mention the weapons ready to be launched from heavy bombers. The advocates of the nuclear freeze argue in other words that the success of a Soviet first strike is so implausible that for the Soviets to attempt it would amount, in the words of President Carter's defense secretary, Harold Brown, to "a cosmic roll of the dice."

To a large extent the debate on August 5 in the House of Representatives involved a test of what the members believed about the state of America's nuclear preparedness. The House Committee Report claimed that the existence of nuclear parity was "confirmed by high-ranking officials in both Republican and Democratic administrations'' and that "none of the present Joint Chiefs of Staff have expressed their willingness to trade overall US capabilities for those of the Soviet Union.''

The dissenting views in the report, signed by six Republicans, reject the freeze and SALT II and insist that all arms control be postponed until there is equality on both sides. The dissent also raises questions about verifiability and alleges that the Soviet Union is a "highly secretive adversary" that "has made deceptive statements during the SALT I and SALT II process concerning ICBM deployment, SLBM quantities, mobile ICBMs and cruise missile ranges.''

The dissenters castigate the nuclear freeze as "dangerous and misleading," claim that it would "lock the United States and our allies into a position of military disadvantage and vulnerability" and that it would mean that the United States and NATO would have no way to offset Soviet nuclear superiority in intermediate range nuclear forces in Europe.''

One of the central themes of the dissent—as it was of those who narrowly prevailed in the debate on the nuclear freeze—was that Congress should not tie the hands of the negotiators in Geneva and that a freeze would give the Soviets no incentive to negotiate reductions.

The nuclear freeze enjoyed broad public support. In every public opinion poll, about two-thirds of all Americans advocated the freeze. It is therefore somewhat astonishing that the U.S. House of Representatives rejected it. A careful study of the debate, which covers 125 pages in the *Congressional Record*, reveals that the fact that ultimately defeated the freeze was the fear that the Soviets were indeed superior in nuclear weapons and that the United States should not freeze, because that would lock the United States into its present position of inferiority. One member of Congress, however, offered the apt analogy that, conceding a slight superiority of the Soviets, the situation is like two adversaries in a room, one with 1,400 pistols and another with 1,200; only negotiations can save either from the first bullet.

The opposition to the freeze was strong. The powerful American Legion and the military-oriented American Security Council opposed the freeze and urged defeat of the resolution of Congressman Clement Zablocki, chairman of the House Foreign Affairs Committee, and the enactment of the White House–endorsed antifreeze amendment of Congressman William Broomfield, ranking Republican member of the House Foreign Affairs Committee. The administration joined in lobbying. It orchestrated stories or leaks about claimed progress in the START talks in Geneva as well as movement in the negotiations about medium-range missiles. The chief U.S. negotiator in Geneva, General Edward Rowney, took time away from the Soviets to phone wavering members of Congress in Washington. The head of the Arms Control and Disarmament Agency—a unit established by Congress to offer an independent and nonpartisan viewpoint in favor of arms control—was everywhere on Capitol Hill urging members of Congress to vote against the nuclear freeze. Ambassadors, the highest Pentagon officials, and the cabinet all lobbied intensely to kill the freeze. A tie vote killing the Broomfield substitute was broken only when two Republicans were induced to change their votes and thus kill the freeze resolution. One hundred fifty-one Republicans were joined by 53 Democrats to make up the final tally of 204. Only 27 Republicans voted for the freeze along with 175 Democrats.

The intense effort that the administration put into killing a resolution that, if it had passed, could have been disregarded as a mere pious wish of one house of Congress reveals the depths of the convictions and the determination on the part of those who believe that the Soviets are preparing to launch a nuclear war. Their convictions are so deep that they use every branch of government to collect and marshal facts to demonstrate the proposition that the Soviets are a deceptive and dangerous foe and that the United States must spend $1.7 trillion in its defense budget over the next four years to outmaneuver them. The rejection of the nuclear freeze was necessary to the administration in its campaign to secure funding for the MX missile, the Trident submarine, the B-1 bomber, and the Cruise missile.

The vigorously antifreeze posture of the Reagan administration can be seen in an address by Secretary of Defense Caspar Weinberger to the American Bar Association on August 11, 1982, in San Francisco. The nuclear freeze proposals, he said, while ''well meaning,'' pose a ''serious threat'' to the ability of the United States to negotiate arms control. The assumption of the secretary's argument is that the Soviet Union is ''almost daily, improving and increasing its nuclear capabilities.'' The offer of a freeze to the Soviets can therefore, in Weinberger's view, be compared to an announcement by a lawyer before a trial that he will not engage in discovery or prepare for the trial. Such a notion, Weinberger says, is ''preposterous'' and would make the lawyer ''guilty of the grossest malpractice.'' The falsity of Weinberger's analogy is self-evident; the arms race, unlike a court trial, is not something anyone can win. The secretary brushes off this fact by claiming that it is ''no good uttering the banal cliché that each superpower has enough to blow each other up.'' But unfortunately the secretary's call for a ''more thorough analysis than that'' fails to bring forth anything except the usual lamentations about the supposed greatly increased nuclear strength of the Soviets.

Will public opinion in favor of the freeze mount to the point that in the Ninety-eighth Congress in 1983--84 some form of the freeze will clear both houses? Or will the fear of the Soviets and the momentum for ''rearming'' America be so intense that the nuclear freeze will fade away? In early 1983 it is impossible to predict the correct answer. But one thing is certain: intense public sentiments in favor of arms control have always had an impact on elected officials in the United States.

The failure of the Ninety-seventh Congress to adopt the nuclear freeze has already prompted the leaders of the freeze movement to conclude that the participants in this movement must have more than slogans. They must be able to quote more than aphorisms about the horrors of nuclear war from Einstein, Eisenhower, or George Kennan. They must be prepared to give a sophisticated explanation of the chart reproduced above, where they must be able to demonstrate that the Russians are not ahead, that there is no "window of vulnerability," and that now is the optimum time for both sides to freeze. It will not be easy to accomplish this objective. If adverse circumstances develop in East-West relations, it might not be possible even to have a meaningful discussion of a nuclear freeze. But the only real failure will be the failure to try. If the nuclear freeze movement fades away or if it is not reborn in some comparable form, the Reagan administration and the Congress will escalate the arms race to new levels where a freeze may be psychologically, strategically, and militarily impossible for both sides. Nuclear weapons and satellites for a war in space could become a reality. Curbs on the proliferation of fissionable material could be further relaxed. Neutron bombs could be multiplied. The five-year plan for a substantial nuclear war issued by the Pentagon in 1982 could be implemented.

Regardless of the status of the nuclear freeze movement, the rhetoric against it will continue to escalate. In August 1982 it rose to the point where Edward N. Luttwak, a professional defense consultant and the author of several books on nuclear weapons, wrote in *Commentary* magazine that "the churchmen who hold that nuclear weapons are *ipso facto* immoral are guilty of a crude ethical illiteracy." Luttwak goes on: "The offense of the antinuclear churchmen is not strategical error, but rather a brutal attack on the most elementary principle of morality, the most basic of religious prescriptions, by which Rabbi Hillel once summarized the entirety of the Bible: what is hateful to you, do not do onto others."

That type of nonsensical onslaught will, it is hoped, be rare, but the proponents of the nuclear freeze must be prepared after their defeat in 1982 for an attack on their intellectual comprehension of the strategic games and gambles of the nuclear age. The nuclear strategists want the game all to themselves. On August 5, 1982, the U.S. House of Representatives for the first time in thirty-seven years discussed and decided a core issue of nuclear arms control. The nuclear planners, the Pentagon, and the State Department felt that their turf had been invaded. Further attempts at such an invasion will be resisted. The Reagan administration probably hopes that it has diffused the nuclear freeze movement, and it may have. Without something concrete to do, such as stopping a war or eliminating the military draft, the momentum for a movement for peace is difficult to maintain.

The architects of the freeze movement, as explained in the paperback *Freeze!* by Senators Edward Kennedy and Mark Hatfield, recognize that "the SALT process was in collapse because the country had no effective constituency for arms control and that there would never be any such constituency without a proposal that people could understand and support." The founders of the freeze movement created a proposal that presumably is comprehensible. The Congress did not find it incomprehensible; what members of the Congress found incomprehensible was the intentions of the Politburo.

The nuclear freeze movement continues to be the clearest, simplest proposal ever made by nonprofessional defense specialists to do something concrete. The action-reaction in the arms race, the mutual buildup of arms, the escalation in American-Soviet nuclear weapons are all portrayed in the literature of the freeze movement in language as simple and as uncomplicated as such complex developments permit.

The freeze movement recalls that it is not proposing something new, since both superpowers agreed in the 1968 Nuclear Non-Proliferation Treaty to the following pledge: "Each of the parties . . . undertakes to pursue negotiations in good faith on effective measures relating to cessation of the nuclear arms race at an early date and to nuclear disarmament . . . and on a treaty on general and complete disarmament under strict and effective international control."

The Senate and the House in 1982 in effect adopted a program initiated by Senator Henry Jackson (D-Washington) and Senator

John Warner (R-Virginia) that calls for a freeze at "equal" levels but only after "sharp" reductions in nuclear arsenals have been made. This plan begins with the assumption that there is presently a "nuclear force imbalance" and that all negotiations for the American side should be deferred until the United States catches up. Advocates of the Kennedy-Hatfield freeze—the essence of the Zablocki proposal—reject this as practically a cover or excuse for another round of arms buildup. At the same time those who concede the desirability of the Jackson-Warner measure admit that a freeze as such is feasible and verifiable—but at a later date. Consequently, the advocates of the nuclear freeze movement stress the point that, as *Freeze!* puts it, "they have agreed to the principle; now they are only haggling over the timing."

Is there some way to combine the two proposals so that there would be a consensus on one program for a nuclear freeze to be adopted by the Congress? Some advocates of the Kennedy-Hatfield freeze would be disinclined to water down a proposal that has already been criticized as too generalized and too unfocused on specific problems. The advocates of the Jackson-Warner proposal would not be prepared to compromise their proposal unless they were forced to do so. They were not so forced in the House on August 5, 1982, when the Broomfield Amendment—the essence of the Jackson-Warner proposal—passed by a vote of 204 to 202. Unless there are strong indications that in 1983 and beyond, the advocates of an immediate nuclear freeze have greater strength in the Congress than they had in 1982, there will be no freeze proposals put to a vote. The danger indeed might well be that the Jackson-Warner proponents would move toward the repeal of SALT I, the abandonment of the ABM treaty, and a return to the unrestrained arms race in which the United States and the Soviet Union were engaged in the 1950s and 1960s.

The future for the architects of the nuclear freeze is difficult and uncertain. One can only hope that the educational efforts of all the organizations that cluster around the freeze movement might be able to make a difference.

The proponents of the freeze, despite the setbacks they have experienced, have a solid case that the freeze and SALT II are far superior to START. The facts are clear:

1. START, which would take at least five years to negotiate, is a limited and very inadequate proposal that reduces each side's total deployed ballistic missiles to 850, deployed intercontinental ballistic missiles to 425, and warheads to roughly six per missile. By contrast the freeze and SALT II are far reaching. The freeze would immediately halt the further testing, production, and deployment of nuclear weapons. Under SALT II some nuclear weapons could be produced, others would be allowed some improvement, still others would be frozen, while others would be prohibited entirely.

2. SALT II limits the Soviet Union Backfire bomber to thirty per year. The freeze cuts it to zero. START does not restrict it at all.

3. Both SALT II and the freeze allow the Soviet Union to retain 308 heavy intercontinental ballistic missiles. START allows 425.

4. The freeze, unlike SALT II or START, prohibits the testing of the multiple-warhead missiles that can destroy American ICBM silos. The freeze thus lowers the confidence in the reliability of these threatening weapons.

5. SALT II allows one new type of ICBM for each side. START allows any number of new types of missile. The freeze ends all new types of missiles.

On most, if not all counts, START is a weak third to either SALT II or the freeze.

How can the nuclear freeze movement translate these conclusions into public policy and law? It may be that the freeze movement will have to concentrate its energies at least in part on resisting the demands of the Pentagon for new weapons of destruction such as binary nerve gas or to resisting the easing of bans on nuclear proliferation or to impeding the buildup of a mentality that accepts nuclear war by spending huge sums of money for civil defense. But the nuclear freeze movement must also concentrate on its core message: It is morally and financially intolerable for America to continue in its customary way of engaging in an arms race with the Soviet Union. A radical departure from the resulting coexistence in terror is imperative. Business as usual cannot go on until the United States does all it can to terminate that which it began at Hiroshima.

In the freeze movement America as a nation experienced that sense of apprehension over an imminent catastrophe that sometimes comes to individuals. At such a moment a person knows that unless things are changed, there will be a disaster like a divorce or the loss of a job or a drastic change in status. The person does not know what should be done but knows profoundly that *something* must be done. That is the mood that gripped those involved in the nuclear freeze movement. George Will, the columnist, called the movement more of a pose than a position. But those in the movement understand that doomsday is coming unless something is changed. They know that the Bomb is like a plague, a pestilence, or an epidemic that—all of the experts agree—cannot be stopped or diverted unless radical action is undertaken. Amid all of the uncertainties surrounding the nuclear freeze movement at the moment, one thing is clear: even the slightest decline in the level of organized and articulated anxiety, anger, and angst in the nuclear freeze movement will permit America to accelerate the nuclear arms race to new and unprecedented levels of threatened violence.

seven

Should the United States Renounce the First Use of Nuclear Weapons?

If the proponents of the nuclear freeze are discouraged at their failure in the Congress in 1982 they feel, nonetheless, that on a related issue—the pledge not to use nuclear weapons on a first-use basis—they may have made some recent progress in raising the consciousness of the American people.

The proposal that the United States forgo the first use of nuclear weapons became popular with the publication in the Spring 1982 issue of *Foreign Affairs* of an article advocating that idea by four persons eminent in the world of nuclear strategy—McGeorge Bundy, special assistant to the President for national security affairs from 1961 to 1966; George F. Kennan, former U.S. ambassador to the Soviet Union; Robert S. McNamara, secretary of defense from 1961 to 1968; and Gerard Smith, chief of the U.S. delegation to the SALT talks from 1969 to 1972.

The concept of forgoing the first use of the nuclear bomb, like the concept of the nuclear freeze, brought out determined and vehement opposition; its opponents claim that the no-first-use doctrine would undermine deterrence and ruin the strategic posture that for almost forty years has brought the longest reign of peace to Europe in modern times.

The four statesmen (called derisively by their critics the "Gang of Four") urged something that no American president has ever agreed to—a pledge never to use nuclear weapons in Europe on a first-strike basis. The pledge would be binding even if the conventional forces of the Warsaw Pact nations were about to overwhelm the massed military might of the NATO nations.

The appeal for a ban on the first use of thermonuclear weapons in Europe had a quality present in the case for the nuclear freeze—the almost desperate feeling that whatever its limitations, it is better than the continued acquiescence in the present nuclear impasse. The proponents of a ban on the first use of the nuclear weapon who wrote the article in *Foreign Affairs* recognized the radical nature of what they were urging. Their article concedes that since August 1949, when the Soviets ended the American monopoly on nuclear weapons, the United States has planned to "use nuclear weapons to defend against aggression in Europe." Circumstances have now changed, the argument goes, so that a no-first-use policy of nuclear weapons should be adopted because in strictly military terms "any other course involves unaccepted risks to the national life that military forces exist to defend." The use of nuclear weapons on a first-strike basis would, in other words, almost certainly impel the Soviet Union to launch a retaliatory response that would devastate American cities.

The advocates of no-first-use recognize the apprehension that this proposal causes in the Federal Republic of Germany. Germany has no nuclear weapons, shares a long common border with the Soviet empire, and in any European conflict would be the first battleground. Germany is therefore much more vulnerable than Great Britain and France, both of whom have nuclear arsenals. If the United States should ever take a no-first-use position, would Germany and the other NATO nations seek to persuade England and France to have their nuclear weapons replace those of the United States? Would the NATO alliance crumble unless the United States pledged to strengthen the conventional forces of NATO to the point that under every imaginable scenario they would be able to resist successfully the fiercest aggression from the Soviet Union?

The four authors of the famous article in *Foreign Affairs* asked if a pledge of "no-*early*-first-use" would suffice. This would mean that there would be a renunciation of nuclear arms except "to fend off a final large-scale conventional defeat." But the authors quickly reject this position as not being clear and simple and, in addition, because exceptions "easily become rules."

The four proponents of the no-first-use position, all of whom served in the Kennedy administration, expressed their fears that "the present unbalanced reliance on nuclear weapons" can if continued, produce alarming changes in the perceptions of the superpowers of each other. And it is in part on that basis that they urge what they concede is a substantial change in something basic in the deterrence theory accepted by every president from the 1950s to the present time. They admit the dangers inherent in such a change but clearly imply that the changes are less threatening than the present situation. They also concede that even if the nuclear powers of the Atlantic Alliance joined in a policy of no-first-use, "no one on either side could guarantee beyond all possible doubt that if conventional warfare broke out on a large scale there would, in fact, be no use of nuclear weapons." But despite this uncertainty the case for no-first-use is still deemed by the four authors to be strong. The implications inherent in the argument for a no-first-use policy are so complex that the four authors candidly admit that "we have only opened this large question, that we have exhausted no aspect of it, and that we may have omitted important elements."

The many critics of the article were quick to point out the "important elements" that were "omitted." The key element was the notion of deterrence. The Bundy-Kennan-McNamara-Smith article recognized deterrence, of course, but affirmed that "in the age of massive thermonuclear overkill it no longer makes sense—if it ever did—to hold the weapons for any purpose than the prevention of their use.'' But critics ask: Does a nuclear weapon deter if those possessing it pledge solemnly to the world that they will not use it unless the other side first unleashes a comparable nuclear device? Will not a no-first-use pledge say to the Warsaw Pact nations that they can plan a massive assault on Western Europe and that the NATO forces will rely only on their concededly inferior conventional arms?

Even the most ardent advocates of nuclear disarmament will have to concede that the article by Mr. Bundy et al. did not stand up completely upon analysis. The case seemed incomplete. It was moreover argued with a certain diffidence that tended to weaken its credibility. It was done in part as a response to the massive antinuclear demonstrations all over Europe. Like the amateurs in the nuclear freeze movement, the four experts in arms control were crying out for something—almost anything— to happen as a way of proclaiming that almost any alternative is better than the present inexorable march to doomsday.

Critics were harsh on the article by Bundy and his colleagues. In the Summer 1982 issue of *Foreign Affairs* four prominent figures in the defense and foreign-policy communities in West Germany—Karl Kaiser, Georg Leber, Alois Mertes, and Franz-Josef Schulze—responded to the article by a vigorous defense of the stability that nuclear deterrence has brought to Germany and to Western Europe. The German reply (referred to here as the Kaiser paper) concedes the paradox of preventing war by threatening a nuclear war but insists that the four American authors advance insufficient evidence to justify their claim that a ''no-first-use policy would render wars less likely. . . .'' The four German authors agree with their American counterparts that ''the kind of Soviet adventurism that would undertake a nuclear first-strike against the United States can be excluded as a serious possibility.'' But the Kaiser article insists that the ''astonishing'' proposal for a no-first-use policy ''would destroy the confidence of Europeans and especially of Germans in the European-American Alliance as a community . . . and would endanger the strategic unity of the Alliance and the security of Western Europe.''

The four American authors furthermore underestimate the political and financial difficulties in establishing a conventional military establishment in the West equal to that of the Warsaw Pact nations. The Kaiser article points moreover to the great difficulties in reducing levels of military strength on both sides, as has been made clear by the as yet unsuccessful negotiations for mutual and balanced force reductions (MBFR) over the past several years.

The German authors candidly reveal their memories of the catastrophes of conventional warfare on their soil and tremble to think that it might occur again in an aggravated form because of the enormously increased power of modern armies. They opt consequently for the present situation, since they see "no alternative to war prevention." They reveal their fears of the Soviet military buildup during the first half of the 1970s—a period during which the West actively sought détente. During those years and since, the Soviets developed and deployed SS-20 missiles in Eastern Europe—weapons below the strategic level and hence not included in SALT. This rocket arsenal has been strengthened by modern systems of short- and medium-range missiles. It was because of this buildup that the NATO nations in 1979 agreed to implement a Western medium-range armament program consisting of 572 Pershing II and Cruise missiles. The Kaiser article recognizes that this decision brought about the antinuclear protest in Western Europe and predicts that this protest "will in all probability remain a permanent characteristic of the political situation in Western Europe for years." But the four German authors see no way to yield to the demands of the antinuclear demonstrators—at least not by renouncing the first use of the nuclear weapon.

The four German authors, unlike Bundy et al., are very forthcoming on the dramatic alterations that would be required in America's military budget if it abandoned the first use of nuclear weapons in Europe and relied exclusively on conventional weapons. The Kaiser article predicts that both Great Britain and the United States would have to introduce the draft and that some

NATO nations would have to extend their period of military service. West Germany would "have to accept on its territory large contingents of additional troops. . . ." And the Federal Republic of Germany "would be transformed into a large military camp for an indefinite period." The German authors shrink from these projections, opening themselves to the charge that they are prepared to condone nuclear warfare in order to curtail military expenditures for the NATO nations and to preserve a certain style of living in West Germany.

The antinuclear groups in the United States have also been reluctant to contemplate the financial and other consequences of withdrawing from Europe the protection that it receives from the threatened first use of nuclear weapons. These groups decline to think about, much less agree to, the very substantial funding that would be required to prevent by conventional means any invasion of Europe by the USSR similar to what Hitler did before and during World War II. Individuals and groups in the United States who are most articulate and aggressive against nuclear weapons are ordinarily also those who desire substantial cutbacks in America's military budget. It will take a good deal of reappraisal on their part before they will be able to announce that in order to rid Europe of the possibility of a nuclear war, they will support additional billions for a strengthening of conventional forces in Europe.

What would it cost to defend Western Europe from the tanks, the aircraft, and the soldiers of the Warsaw Pact nations? The very facts underlying this question are in dispute. The experts are not in agreement. Even the issues involved are not entirely clear.

In the search for an answer to that question the total outlays of both sides are relevant but are not necessarily helpful. NATO has always outspent the Warsaw Pact. In 1980 NATO military spending was $241 billion, compared with $202 billion for the Warsaw Pact countries. About one-fourth of the latter figure, however, was spent for Soviet forces directed against China. The following chart contains all the relevant numbers, but even the best-informed military experts are not in agreement on their full meaning.

At a Glance: Military Resources of NATO, Warsaw Pact, & People's Republic of China			
	NATO	Warsaw Pact	China
Population	575,000,000	376,600,000	1,034,400,000
GNP	$5,727 Billion	$2,019 Billion	$552 Billion
Military Spending	$241 Billion	$202 Billion	$57 Billion
Military Manpower	4.9 million	4.8 million	4.8 million
Strategic Nuclear Weapons	10,200	7,800	Several hundred
Theater Nuclear Weapons	21,000	10-15,000	N.A.
Tanks	28,000	63,000	11,600
Anti-tank Missiles	300,000+	N.A.	N.A.
Other Armored Vehicles	53,000	83,000	4,000
Heavy Artillery	15,200	24,000	18,000
Combat Aircraft	10,500	10,850	6,100
Helicopters	12,350	4,500	350
Major Surface Warships	403	281	32
Attack Submarines (incl. cruise missile subs)	224	298	104

N.A.—Data Not Available
Source: 1980–81 Dept. of Defense, IISS, CIA, CDI.

How difficult and expensive would the defense of Europe be if the United States and NATO renounced the use of nuclear weapons on a first-use basis? The answer to that question depends on a wide variety of assumptions. The *London Economist* for July 31, 1982, attempted an answer but prefaced its attempt by stating that the "only predictable thing about war is that nothing is entirely predictable." The *Economist* estimated that the total costs for resisting a Soviet invasion of Europe and for avoiding nuclear war would mean that the United States would have to increase the percentage of what it is spending on defense of its gross national product from 5.8 percent to 7.5 percent. West Germany would have to spend 4.2 percent of its gross national product instead of its present 3.4 percent, and France would be required to increase its military costs from 4.2 percent to 5.0 percent of its gross national product. The *Economist* tries to justify what it concedes to be its "optimism about the relative small extra cost" by calculating the costs, among other items, of having several thousand more American soldiers combat-ready either in Europe or in the United States prepared to arrive in Europe by air within forty-eight hours after the attack from the East. Additional costs would include an increase in NATO's antisubmarine forces in the Atlantic. These costs would be necessary to keep open the sea lanes in order to prevent a long war under massive Russian submarine attacks. In addition, vast sums for storage in Europe of heavy equipment, not now available, would be required. Added millions would be needed to have large numbers of conscripts prepared to fight in Europe within hours of a conventional assault from the Warsaw Pact nations.

The survey by the *Economist* is based on consultations with generals, admirals, and defense specialists on both sides of the Atlantic and both sides of the Iron Curtain. Its conclusions are open to challenge as somewhat speculative. But its estimate of America's bill for the denuclearization of Europe is probably as accurate as is possible. The *Economist* concludes with the tough and unavoidable question, "Is the anti-nuclear movement willing to help stump up the money it would take to achieve security without the weapons we all wish had never been invented?"

Antinuclear advocates must therefore confront some thorny questions. Do they hold that the United States must deem NATO its first line of defense and therefore be prepared to prevent or roll back an invasion of that continent as occurred in World War I and World War II? If the defense of Europe is a moral and treaty obligation of the United States, should that obligation be carried out without the use or protection of the nuclear umbrella? If a pledge of no-first-use were made by the United States with respect to the European theater, could this result in a sweep of Warsaw Pact nations over Europe in a blitzkrieg? Would the resulting Soviet occupation be so firm and entrenched that it would be virtually impossible to dislodge?

Again the question returns to the intentions of the Soviets. The anti-Soviet feeling has been so profound, persistent, and pervasive in America for some thirty years that one feels inhibited about saying something favorable concerning the Soviets. For a politician any favorable reference to the Soviets is dangerous. For others any kindly feelings toward the Soviet Union are looked upon as naive, ill founded, or the result of being duped.

The question of a nuclear freeze of some sort is not likely to be resolved absent some new feeling towards "the other side." At the present time—and more so as the result of the harsh rhetoric of President Reagan and his administration—the Soviets are characterized almost as irrational monsters who would do anything illegal or immoral to achieve their malicious objectives. The most that hard-line anti-Soviet observers in the United States will concede is that the asserted evil intentions attributed to the Soviet Union probably reside in their leaders and not in their people.

The proponents of the nuclear freeze try to counter by assuming or asserting that Russian parents are just as anxious as American parents to preserve the lives of their children and grandchildren and that the United States is unjustified in continuing to think that Soviet intentions are barbaric and that Russian leaders are really less than human. The freeze proponents do not deny the harshness of what the Soviets are doing in Poland and Afghanistan, but they want to see this in the light of what the United States did in Vietnam. There is not, in other words, a clear confrontation going on between good and evil. The intentions on both sides are multifaceted, mixed, and mysterious.

The objectives of the nuclear freeze movement were embraced in a somewhat different way in the attempts during 1982 to persuade the United States to renounce a first use of nuclear weapons. Neither the freeze nor the no-first-use drive can claim any specific political victories. Presumably, both movements raised the consciousness of countless persons. But the resistance to the freeze and to the no-first-use proposal prompted those terrified by the possibility of a nuclear war to turn to another inquiry as a possible source of hope: Does international law make the use of nuclear weapons illegal? If so, why is such law not enforced? If not, could international law be clarified and strengthened so that the use of nuclear weapons under all circumstances would be made a violation of international law? It is to that topic—of special and deep interest to those newly established groups of lawyers for nuclear control—to which we now direct our attention.

eight

Are Nuclear Weapons Illegal?

If the proponents of the nuclear freeze have been unsuccessful in persuading the Congress or the country to halt all new development and deployment of atomic weapons, the jurists and the courts of the world have been similarly unsuccessful in devising national or international laws that are perceived as binding prohibitions on the use of nuclear bombs. To the nations that rely on the nuclear deterrent the seemingly stringent bans on bombing civilian populations that exist in several areas of international law do not appear to make their conduct illegal.

The legal silence about nuclear weapons has been so profound that in 1982 groups of lawyers, following the example of physicians and scientists, organized to bring the skills of the legal profession to bear on the problems caused by the presence of nuclear weapons. Unfortunately, as Professor Richard Falk of Princeton University, an eminent expert in international law, confessed in 1981, "this momentous topic has received virtually no attention from international lawyers." He further confesses in a paper *Nuclear Weapons and International Law*, published by the Princeton University Center of International Studies, that from the dawn of the nuclear age "almost nothing was done to incorporate into the laws of war an authoritative prohibition on the use of nuclear weapons.'' The situation is made even worse by the fact that the opinion has grown within the legal community that the traditional principles for the conduct of war agreed to in the Geneva and The Hague covenants and treaties were invalidated during World War II because of the practice of the Allies in bombing in ways that appeared to contravene international standards.

International law has never really been able to categorize or condemn what was done at Hiroshima and Nagasaki. In the period of nearly forty years since the world's first and only atomic detonations only one court of law has ruled on the legality of what the United States did on August 6 and 9, 1945. In May 1955 five Japanese citizens brought suit against the Japanese government for injuries sustained as a result of the bombings of Hiroshima and Nagasaki. On December 7, 1963 the District Court of Tokyo delivered a lengthy decision ruling that the bombings had violated international law. The plaintiffs in the *Shimoda* case described for the court the scene they saw: ''People in rags of hanging skin wandered about and lamented aloud among dead bodies. It was an extremely sad sight beyond the description of a burning hell, and beyond all imagination of anything heretofore known in human history.'' They claimed that what was done to them violated all of the rules of law set forth in the conventions of Geneva and The Hague, which forbid the destruction of all property except that which clearly belongs to a military installation. The plaintiffs also claimed that the Japanese government, in waiving all claims of its nationals in the peace treaty with the United States, wrongfully deprived them of claims based on violations of international law.

The government of Japan defended against the lawsuit by asserting that the atomic bombs were new inventions and hence were not covered by the customary or the conventional rules of the international law of war. But the Tokyo District Court, after reviewing the devastation done at Hiroshima and Nagasaki, concluded that the atomic bomb ''cannot for a moment be compared with bombs of the past.'' The court ruled that the legal standards developed prior to the creation of the atomic bomb by analogy or by clear inference forbid nuclear weapo:1s. Citing The Hague Rules of Land Warfare, which only permit the bombing of a defended city near the battlefield, the Tokyo court held that the indiscriminate bombing of Hiroshima and Nagasaki—cities with no concentration of military objectives—was an act contrary to international law.

The court went on to argue that the plaintiffs were entitled to damages under Japanese municipal law since they had been injured by a violation of international law—a law accepted by the Japanese government. The decision, by consent of both parties to the suit, was not appealed.

For two generations lawyers have sought to maximize the impact of the *Shimoda* ruling. It is not, however, a precedent. It is contrary to the 1927 *Lotus* decision of the Permanent Court of International Justice, which held that a weapon can be legally used in war unless its use is expressly prohibited by an international convention. The *Lotus* decision is the official position of the United States as expressed in its field manuals for the armed services. Article 613 of the Law of Naval Warfare, issued in 1955, reads: ''There is at present no rule of international law expressly prohibiting states from the use of nuclear weapons in warfare. In the absence of expressed prohibition, the use of such weapons against enemy combatants and other military objectives is permitted.''

Article 613 refers, however, to other sections of the Law of Naval Warfare that point out the contradictions in the broad validation of nuclear weapons. Article 621(a), for instance, prohibits ''the wanton destruction of cities, towns or villages, or any devastation not justified by military necessity. . . .'' The contradiction is further dramatized by the directive of Article 621(c) that ''bombardment for the sole purpose of terrorizing the civilian population is prohibited.''

The ambivalence demonstrated in America's contradictory approach to the legality of nuclear weapons was not present on

November 24, 1961, when the United States voted against Resolution 1653 in the United Nations General Assembly. This resolution, which condemned all nuclear war as a violation of international law, was adopted by a vote of fifty-five to twenty, with twenty-six countries abstaining.

Basing its conclusions on past prohibitions by international agreements condemning mass destruction as being contrary to the laws of humanity and the principles of international law, Section 1 of the Declaration on the Prohibition of the Use of Nuclear and Thermo-Nuclear Weapons declared that:

1. The use of nuclear and thermo-nuclear weapons is contrary to the spirit, letter and aims of the United Nations and, as such, a direct violation of the Charter of the United Nations;
2. The use of nuclear and thermo-nuclear weapons would exceed even the scope of war and cause indiscriminate suffering and destruction to mankind and civilization and, as such, is contrary to the rules of international law and to the laws of humanity;
3. The use of nuclear and thermo-nuclear weapons is a war directed not against an enemy or enemies alone but also against mankind in general, since the peoples of the world not involved in such a war will be subjected to all the evils generated by the use of such weapons;
4. Any state using nuclear and thermo-nuclear weapons is to be considered as violating the Charter of the United Nations, as acting contrary to the laws of humanity and as committing a crime against mankind and civilization.

The United States was joined in its rejection of this statement by the United Kingdom, France, and China; the Soviet Union and India voted for it.

The UN General Assembly in 1980 again demonstrated the international consensus by declaring the use of nuclear weapons to be a ''violation of the Charter of the United Nations and a crime against humanity.'' The same document concluded that the ''use or threat of use of nuclear weapons should therefore be prohibited, pending nuclear disarmament.''

The rejection by the United States of the solemn affirmation by humanity of the illegality of nuclear weapons can hardly be encouraging to the lawyers of the United States who more and more desire to utilize the law to make the use of nuclear weapons unacceptable.

The ineffectiveness of the law of war in controlling atomic weapons is tragically clear. There is, however, a gathering consensus among legal scholars and jurists that the *Shimoda* decision was correct and that the whole thrust of prenuclear international law goes in the direction of condemning the use and even the possession of nuclear weapons.

The Martens Clause, for example, to the Hague Convention of 1907 spells out a restriction on nations at war:

> "Until a more suitable code of laws can be drawn up, the high contracting parties deem it expedient to declare that, in cases not covered by the rules adopted by them, the inhabitants and the belligerents remain under the protection and governance of the general principles of the law of nations, derived from the usages established among civilized peoples from the laws of humanity, and from the dictates of the public conscience."

The four Geneva Conventions of 1949 strengthened this principle by reaffirming (after Hiroshima, it should be noted) the fundamental distinction between competent and noncompetent. In addition, Article 35(3) seemed to outlaw nuclear weapons with this mandate: "It is prohibited to employ methods and means of warfare which are intended, or may be expected, to cause widespread, long-term and severe damage to the natural environment."

The Nuremberg principles accepted into international law by the General Assembly on December 11, 1946, also appeared to outlaw nuclear war. Article 6(c) defines crimes against humanity as the "extermination of a civilian population, before or during a war." This approach became a part of the Genocide Convention, which now has entered into force with the ratification of more than one hundred nations—a group that does not include the United States.

The basic principles of traditional international law seem to apply to nuclear weapons. But clearly they have generally not been applied. This phenomenon may be the result—as the late Hans Morgenthau remarked—of the fact that the thing we call nuclear "war" is really not war at all in any traditional sense and the devices that we call nuclear "weapons" transcend any customary or accepted definition of a weapon. Nuclear war, in other words, is so monstrous that none of the categories ever devised by international jurists really apply. The concepts of war and weapons as understood by the lawyers who wrote the restrictions in international law do not really fit the type of devastation that results from the use of nuclear weapons.

Some lawyers may despair of using their discipline to try to bring about a rule of law that will govern the nations that possess the bomb. They would tend to agree with those who say that the very possession of nuclear weapons violates the very essence of anything mankind has ever devised for the control of war. Their sentiments were expressed in *Foreign Affairs* in 1973 by a person about to become director of the Arms Control and Disarmament Agency, Fred Iklé: ". . . our method for preventing nuclear war rests on a form of warfare universally condemned since the dark ages—the mass killing of hostages."

If this is a reliable description of what nuclear war is based on, it seems clear that hopes to apply the rules of The Hague, Geneva, and Nuremberg are forlorn if not illusory.

What then can lawyers do? Despite the supralegal or nonlegal atmosphere in which the use of nuclear weapons is now discussed, the fact is that of all the potential forces—religion, morality, humanitarianism—law probably has an appeal and an attraction that is unique. Both the United States and the Soviet Union share in large part a Western tradition of jurisprudence that derives at least in part from Aristotle and the Stoics. It has been enriched and enhanced by Judaism and Christianity and by the natural-law theories of the Middle Ages. It has been greatly strengthened by the rich developments in common law or Anglo-American law over the past eight centuries. Marxism, moreover, has never repudiated the integrity and centrality of this law except insofar as it has been used to justify what Marxism would call capitalistic exploitation. The law of Western civilization, therefore, has a very significant potential to be the force by which modern man will be able to unravel the forces of lawlessness that have permitted the superpowers to be so convinced of the need of atomic weapons that they have discarded and almost forgotten those wise restraints on the exercise of armed violence that civilized mankind over a period of several decades developed for nonnuclear weapons. If these restraints cannot in the nature of things be applied in any meaningful way to the use of nuclear weapons, governments and the legal profession should say so. If all of these rules and restraints have some useful applicability to the conduct of nuclear warfare, they should be revitalized and reinstated as the norms by which the United States will be guided in the use of its 30,000 nuclear weapons.

It is humiliating for lawyers in the United States to review the disregard of law that has characterized America's handling of nuclear weapons. The United States has denied any culpability for the victims of Hiroshima and Nagasaki, voted against the condemnation of nuclear war in the United Nations, refused to sign the genocide treaty, and in its official Pentagon manuals teaches its military personnel that nuclear wars are not illegal.

In 1982, for the first time in the nuclear age, lawyers came together to form groups like the Lawyers Alliance for Nuclear Arms Control. This group, with other units, was responsible for the first pronouncement on nuclear war by the American Bar Association. In San Francisco in August 1982 the organized bar of some quarter of a million attorneys agreed to a somewhat bland but significant statement on nuclear war. The preamble of the statement proposed by the Massachusetts Bar Association and other legal groups noted that "nuclear war may mean the end of civilization as we know it, and an end to the law, institutions and constitutional framework which lawyers are sworn to defend and uphold.''

The statement urged that the U.S. policy on nuclear arms control be based on the following principles:

1. It is of the greatest urgency and importance that the nuclear powers pursue serious and sustained negotiations to end the nuclear arms race and to reduce the number of nuclear weapons.
2. The nuclear powers should further pursue the development of agreements facilitating communication and coordination in order to reduce the possibility of nuclear war through error or misunderstanding.
3. The nuclear powers must urgently strive to prevent further proliferation of nuclear weapons.
4. The nuclear powers should avoid conduct and rhetoric that invite nuclear confrontation and obscure their mutual interests in reducing the risks of nuclear war.
5. Efforts to achieve nuclear superiority escalate the nuclear arms race and increase the risk of nuclear war.

Lawyers have to face several legal-moral issues of mind-shattering difficulty. Can the very concept of deterrence be legally justified? Strategic deterrence threatens mass destruction for possibly a large portion of humanity for the sole purpose of preserving the territorial integrity of some of the nations of Western Europe. Is such a threat compatible with the basic premises of the civil and criminal laws of civilized nations? Can one nation prepare itself to kill millions of people and decimate a substantial part of the world just to protect its own physical integrity? Is such a position—which the United States has accepted—reconcilable with the fundamental rules of war, which the United States has also accepted?

Is nuclear war, furthermore, consistent with the clear mandate placed in the Constitution by the founding fathers that the Congress and the Congress alone has the power to declare war? That constitutional mandate was clarified in 1973 in the War Powers Resolution passed over the veto of President Richard Nixon.

That law, enacted to prevent any further undeclared wars like Vietnam, requires the president to consult the Congress before committing military personnel to countries where hostilities are likely to occur. It also provides for specific timetables according to which Congress can terminate United States military involvement initiated by a president. But the law designed to protect both the power of Congress under the Constitution to declare war and the power of the president to protect the safety of the nation does not regulate the president's power to act on his own by starting a nuclear war. In the lengthy discussions in Congress and in the country about the War Powers Resolution, no way was found to require the president before starting a nuclear war to conform with the Constitution. The authors of that Constitution, having seen over many generations the British unilaterally declare wars, made it clear beyond doubt that this awesome power in the United States would be diffused among members of both houses of Congress. Is it possible to retain that provision while permitting the president the right to initiate a nuclear war for offensive or defensive objectives?

Is there some way, moreover, by which lawyers, with all of their skills in negotiation and compromise, could intervene to stop the action-reaction syndrome that has for many years escalated the arms race? One of the most recent examples of this built-in cause of the momentum in the nuclear arms race is the present superiority by the United States in the development and deployment of Cruise missiles. In December 1982 the United States began to deploy 8,000 Cruise missiles—38 on B-52s and B-1s, up to 4,000 on ships and submarines, and 464 that are ground-launched in Western Europe. The Soviets will not have this weapon for another five or even ten years. These missiles are not covered by the SALT process since they are tactical and not strategic. But the threat that they pose to the Soviets is so clear and overwhelming that the Kremlin simply has to alter its military and civilian priorities in order to be able to deploy the Cruise missile as soon as possible.

Lawyers, more than most Americans, feel frustrated that the

elaborate chess game of negotiations in the SALT process was interrupted and its momentum destroyed. No similar momentum is apparent in the START talks in Geneva. Lawyers, anxious to employ their skills at fence mending and mediating, long to break into the deadlocked situation that exists between the superpowers. It will not be easy. But the victories that lawyers have had in the history of America gives reason for hope that they can save the United States from the immense folly of once again employing the nuclear bomb. Lawyers wrote the Declaration of Independence, fashioned the U.S. Constitution, framed the legal instruments to heal the nation after the Civil War, created the Civil Rights Acts of the 1960s, and authored the laws for the environmental revolution of the 1970s. They are now called to be the moral architects of a process by which the United States will extricate itself from the frightening predicament of being the world's principal protagonist in the origin and the perpetuation of the nuclear arms race.

America has endured two great crucial legal-moral crises—its break with England in the American Revolution and its abolition of slavery following the Civil War. Its third crisis—greater than the other two because it involves all of humanity—is its desired escape from the nuclear nightmare. Lawyers were the symbol makers and the wordsmiths at the time of the revolution and of the Emancipation Proclamation. They are uniquely qualified and will be indispensably necessary in assisting America to overcome the horror of being the creator of the nuclear age.

Law is often grounded on moral values and these values not infrequently derive at least ultimately from religious and scriptural ideals. Consequently, lawyers and jurists, anxious to bring about a fundamental alteration in the way the United States regards nuclear weapons, will do well to heed the ever more abundant counsel of religious persons and groups—a topic to which we now turn.

nine

Is Nuclear
Deterrence Immoral
in Catholic Tradition?

From the beginning of the nuclear age the churches have been aghast at the level of violence already unleashed and at the frightening potential of the violence that is threatened. In 1981 the Fellowship of Reconciliation issued a forty-page brochure containing most of the major pronouncements of ecclesiastical groups on the bomb. The statements almost try to outdo each other in the vehemence of their denunciation of nuclear weapons. Perhaps the strongest of all condemnations by a major religious group is a 170-page report issued in August 1982 by a panel of the Church of England. The report proposed that Great Britain phase out its Polaris nuclear submarine missiles and drop plans to accept deployment of U.S. Cruise missiles. The conclusion that Great Britain is morally required to undertake unilateral disarmament is scheduled to be debated in the spring of 1983 by the General Synod of the Anglican Church.

One can only speculate as to whether the nuclear arms race would have been less catastrophic if more persons had followed the directives of the churches or whether the statements of the church-related groups were too general to have any specific effect on the conduct of the nations that possessed atomic weapons. In any event, the churches have preached for almost forty years against thermonuclear war, but the nuclear situation has worsened and deteriorated—almost without a single sign of improvement at any time. The World Council of Churches in May 1982 issued a report on a conference on nuclear weapons in Amsterdam, summing up what the churches have been saying for two generations. After recognizing that ''there is no Christian consensus on the subject of war as such,'' the World Council of Churches nonetheless concluded that ''we wish to state unequivocally that nuclear warfighting is morally wrong, whatever the circumstances.''

Comparable statements can be cited from Catholic sources. As early as 1954 Pope Pius XII told the World Medical Association: ''*Atomic,* biological and chemical warfare involves such an extension of evil that it entirely escapes from the control of man and its use must be rejected as immoral. Here, there would no longer be a question of one 'defense' . . . but the pure and simple annihilation of all human life within the radius of action. This is not permitted *for any reason whatsoever.*'' (Emphasis supplied.)

The same sentiments are found in the address of Pope John Paul II in Coventry, England, in May 1982 in these words: ''Today, the scale of horror of modern war—whether nuclear or not—makes it totally unacceptable as a means of settling differences between nations. War should belong to the tragic past, to history; it should find no place on humanity's agenda for the future.''

The same pontiff said almost the same thing on the occasion of his visit to Hiroshima on February 25, 1981: ''In the past, it was possible to destroy a village, a town, a region, even a country. Now it is the whole planet that has come under threat. This fact should finally compel everyone to face a basic moral consideration; from now on, it is only through a conscious and through a deliberate policy that humanity can survive.''

The most quoted papal condemnation of war was made by Pope John XXIII on Easter Sunday in 1963 in his encyclical *Pacem in terris.* He stated that "nuclear weapons should be banned. . . . It is hardly possible to imagine that in the atomic era war could be used as an instrument of peace." It was this sweeping statement along with expressions of faith and hope that prompted the entire world to greet *Pacem in terris* with more exultant joy than any other papal message in memory. It reminds one of Gandhi's adage that "human nature is one and therefore unfailingly responds to the advances of love." It may be that Pope John in his view of the Soviets was more responsive than most to Paul's injunction to "disarm malice with kindness" (Romans 12:21).

It is not certain that the letter or spirit of *Pacem in terris* is fully reflected in the twenty-five hundred words on the morality of war issued by the 2,200 bishops of Vatican II in December 1965. A comparison of the relevant excerpts from *Pacem in terris* with the statement of Vatican II on war shows that the Vatican II pronouncement tends to be narrow, legalistic, and guarded. It is, nonetheless, the firmest condemnation of nuclear war ever issued by the Catholic church. Its central points are immensely significant. The document that contains the statement on war, the Pastoral Constitution on the Church in the Modern World, specifically condemns nuclear war whether offensive or defensive, since it affirms that "Any act of war aimed indiscriminately at the destruction of entire cities or of extensive areas along with their population is a crime against God and man himself. It merits unequivocal and unhesitating condemnation."

The council similarly condemned "as most infamous" those actions "designed for the methodical extermination of an entire people, nation or ethnic minority."

The question left unanswered by Vatican II, however, was this: How can the possession of intercontinental ballistic missiles, designed precisely to achieve morally forbidden objectives, be deemed a moral act? This question was raised by the late Cardinal Joseph Ritter during the fourth session of Vatican

II. In his intervention, which was seen only by the members of a conciliar subcommission, Cardinal Ritter asked that the very possession of the arms required for a total war be categorically condemned. The statement of Cardinal Ritter, published shortly after his death, deserves attention. The cardinal asked this question:

> The possession of those arms which actually constitute the "balance of terror," even those which are aimed exclusively at deterring an adversary, already involve the intention—conditional, perhaps, but effective—of using those arms: for possession without any intention of use would deter no one, would effect nothing. From the very nature of these arms, their enormous quantity and distribution, it can be seen what kind and how great a destruction is already projected. How then are we able to condemn every intention of destroying cities and at the same time, at least in part, approve the balance of terror?

Cardinal Ritter's conclusion in the same document is this: "I believe, therefore, that there should be an absolute condemnation of the possession of arms which involve the intention of the grave peril of total war."

The Second Vatican Council did not really respond to the thrust of Cardinal Ritter's challenge. The council fathers made some attempt to answer the question but in the end left it unresolved. The council states that the "defensive strength of any nation is considered to be dependent upon its capacity for immediate retaliation against an adversary. Hence this accumulation of arms, which increases each year, also serves, in a way heretofore unknown, as a deterrent to possible enemy attack." The council goes on to concede that "many regard this state of affairs as the most effective way by which peace of a sort can be maintained between nations at the present time." But we are not told who are the "many" who regard the present state of affairs as "the *most* effective way" to maintain peace. These statements seem in fact to contradict another section of the document where the council states that "the arms race is an utterly treacherous step for humanity, and one which injures the poor to an intolerable degree.''

It would be pleasant to be able to record a worldwide implementation of what Vatican II said about war by Catholic communities around the world. Hierarchies did speak out, Christian peace groups grew in size and influence, and the fear of nuclear war, so vividly portrayed in the words of Vatican II, entered into the minds and hearts of millions of Catholics and others. But the arms race grew faster.

The Catholic bishops of the United States took up the message on war of Vatican II in their annual statements in 1966 and 1968. In its 1968 letter the American hierarchy referred to the topic—which is still troubling them and the world—the morality of the possession of weapons that cannot be utilized. The hierarchy did not itself seek to ban the possession but urged that the United States cease trying to maintain ''nuclear superiority'' since ''any effort to achieve superiority leads to ever higher levels of armaments as it forces the side with the lesser capability to maintain its superiority.''

The bishops in 1968 also expressed their misgivings about the advisability of the then current efforts to build the ABM. The 1968 episcopal statement also raised the most serious questions about America's continuing involvement in the war in Vietnam and questioned whether the tragic losses could possibly be proportionate to any gain that might be obtained.

The Catholic bishops spoke about nuclear war again in 1976; they clearly stated that ''not only is it wrong to attack civilian populations but it is also wrong to threaten to attack them as part of a strategy of deterrence.'' But it was not until 1981 that they commissioned a group to prepare for them a comprehensive study on the ethical issues surrounding nuclear war. Originally scheduled for debate and decision in November 1982, the statement will now be finalized in 1983.

The Catholic community in America has always felt a sense of guilt over the bombing of Hiroshima and Nagasaki—two heavily Catholic communities in a non-Christian nation. Catholics recognize, moreover, that since they make up 24 percent of the population and 30 percent of the armed forces, they have a responsibility to make themselves heard. This responsibility is deepened by the presence within Catholicism of a set of moral principles regarding a just war that are more developed and sophisticated than anything comparable in non-Catholic religious traditions.

The availability of those traditional norms has not, however, been notably helpful to Catholics in assessing the morality of nuclear warfare. The customary norms for a just war are straightforward. Before any war can be morally justified the following conditions must be fulfilled:

1. The war must be declared by a legitimate public authority possessing the power to do so;
2. A real injury must have been suffered;
3. The damage likely to follow from the war cannot be disproportionate to the injury suffered;
4. There must be a reasonable hope of success;
5. Every possible means of peaceful settlement must have been exhausted;
6. Those prosecuting the war must have a moral intention;
7. Only legitimate and moral means may be utilized in prosecuting the war.

These norms, originated by Saint Augustine, refined by Aquinas, and synthesized by Francisco de Vitoria, seem to be impossible to fulfill in any nuclear war. How can the requirement of proportionality ever be fulfilled, since the death and destruction will inevitably so far surpass whatever political objective that may be sought? How can there be ahead of time any "reasonable hope of success," since neither can actually "succeed"? One can argue that Vatican II meant to set aside those rules when it mandated that war must be viewed "with an entirely new attitude."

If, therefore, there is questionable validity and viability in the centuries-old norms on a just war, what norms can be utilized in evaluating the morality of a nuclear clash? It may be that Vatican

II applied the just-war test and concluded, as we have seen, that nuclear war may never be allowed whether it is employed offensively or defensively or on a first- or second-strike basis. The only question left open by Vatican II is whether a nation can morally continue the possession of nuclear weapons that it may not morally use.

That question was addressed by the U.S. Catholic bishops in 1979 when Cardinal John Krol of Philadelphia, testifying officially for the U.S. Catholic Conference on behalf of SALT II before the U.S. Senate, stated that "not only the use of strategic nuclear weapons but also the declared intent to use them involved in our deterrence policy is wrong. This explains the Catholic dissatisfaction with nuclear deterrence and the urgency of the Catholic demand that the nuclear arms race be reversed."

The demand for a reversal is urgent and "as long as there is hope of this occurring, Catholic moral theology is willing, while negotiations proceed, to tolerate the possession of nuclear weapons for deterrence as the lesser of two evils. If that hope were to disappear, the moral attitude of the Catholic Church would almost certainly have to shift to one of uncompromising condemnation of both the use and the possession of such weapons."

The only issue still unresolved, therefore, is the nature of the "hope" for a reversal of the arms race that justifies the "toleration" of the possession of atomic weapons that can never be used. Will this "toleration" of the lesser evil—that is, the possession of super lethal weapons—cease to be allowed if the greater evil—the threat of attack—becomes more and more dubious? How does one assess the malice in each of these two evils? What if leaders of the Soviet Union expressly state, as they did in 1982, that they will never use the nuclear weapon on a first-strike basis? Those who agree with the Catholic teaching that the use, the threatened use, and the possession of nuclear weapons is immoral must regularly continue to evaluate the depths of the greater evil, since its existence and its threat is the only justification for the possession of the lesser evil.

Cardinal Krol's statement said that Catholics may tolerate the possession of nuclear weapons "while negotiations proceed." There were no negotiations during the first several months of the Reagan administration. Why, moreover, should anyone be able to rely on negotiations when not a single weapon has been destroyed by negotiation in the whole history of the nuclear era? The United States manufactures three more nuclear weapons each day—1,300 per year. What should Catholics do if an administration announced the cancellation of all negotiations, stating that the Soviets are not willing to bargain in good faith? Even more complicated, what should Catholics do if the Kremlin broke off talks, claiming that the White House was not sincere?

The U.S. Catholic bishops became more concerned with the issue of nuclear war in 1981 for the same reasons that the Western world did. In 1980 President Carter issued Presidential Directive 59, which expanded the range of targets of nuclear weapons beyond the urban-industrial community that had been the focus of strategic planning for two decades. Presidential Directive 59 seemed to modify the previous policy of "mutually assured destruction" by suggesting that nuclear weapons were to be used to win a war and not just for deterrence. In 1981 Vice-President George Bush stated that a nuclear war is "winnable"; at the same time the Pentagon appeared to be preparing to strengthen the offensive capabilities of nuclear strategy.

The European demonstrations against nuclear war undoubtedly aroused the Catholic bishops to a greater concern over America's nuclear policy. The protests in Europe were supported, even initiated, by a wide variety of ecclesiastical and other organizations. The Catholic communities in Europe, along with their bishops, were deeply involved. The religious press in Europe pointed to the responsibility of the Catholics in America as the largest single religious denomination in the nation that started the nuclear madness. One religious periodical noted that at Vatican II 10 percent of the bishops attending came from the United States but that they gave little leadership on the nuclear issue.

For whatever reasons, the Catholic hierarchy in 1981 entered a pilgrimage that might well lead them to an active condemnation of a central premise of America's defense policy. In 1981 over 40 bishops joined in statements vigorously critical of U.S. nuclear policy. In March 1981, 17 bishops, members of Pax Christi, asked Archbishop Joseph Bernardin, chairman of a committee established by the bishops to examine war-peace issues, if there could be any morally justifiable warfare in view of the savagery of modern weaponry. In August Archbishop John Roach of Minneapolis–Saint Paul and Chairman of the National Conference of Catholic Bishops, reiterated the conference's previous criticism of the neutron warhead. Also in August Bishop Leroy Matthiesen of Amarillo, Texas, counseled Catholics in his diocese to disengage themselves from work in places in his diocese where nuclear weapons were finally assembled; he was later joined by the 12 Catholic bishops of Texas. In October Archbishop John Quinn of San Francisco supported the nuclear freeze movement—as did at later times 133 of the nation's 280 active bishops. Archbishop Quinn also opposed cooperation in civilian defense measures, since they tend to presume survivability in nuclear war.

In November Archbishop Roach in his presidential address at the annual bishops' meeting declared that the Church must act since the "secular debate is openly discussing the use of limited weapons and winning nuclear wars."

The series of initiatives for peace taken by the bishops in 1981 prompted Monsignor Vincent A. Yzermans, former information director of the U.S. Catholic Conference, to write in the *New York Times* on November 14, 1981, that the episcopal activity on nuclear war was "the most significant revolution within the Catholic Church since Lord Baltimore's contingent of Catholics disembarked on Maryland shores in 1634." He predicted an "explosion between church and state that will make the abortion issue, the school-aid controversy and the tax-exempt status of churches look like a child's sparklers on the Fourth of July." Summarizing the proliferation of antinuclear episcopal pronouncements in 1981, Richard McCormick, S.J., noted moral theologian, remarked in *Theological Studies* for March 1982 that "religious leadership in the United States, especially Catholic, is on a collision course with the U.S. government. That just may be the best thing to happen to both in a long time."

But perhaps the most extraordinary occurrence in 1981 was the endorsement of unilateral disarmament by Archbishop Raymond Hunthausen of Seattle. In a very moving address on June 12 to the Pacific Northwest Synod of the Lutheran church, he expressed regret at not speaking out earlier against nuclear arms and the "nearby construction of the Trident submarine base . . . the first-strike nuclear doctrine which Trident represents." He startled his community and no doubt outraged some by stating that the "Trident is the Auschwitz of Puget Sound."

He acted, he revealed, because "politics is . . . powerless to overcome the demonic in its midst." He cites the words of Christ in Mark (8:34) that persons desirous of following Christ must "take up the cross." To Archbishop Hunthausen "one obvious meaning of the cross is unilateral disarmament." He concedes the force of the argument against this unilateral course but then poses this telling challenge: "To ask one's country to relinquish its security in arms is to encourage risk—a more reasonable risk than constant nuclear escalation—but a risk nevertheless."

He goes on with these moving words: "I am struck by how much more terrified we Americans often are by talk of disarmament than by the march to nuclear war. We whose nuclear arms terrify millions around the globe are terrified by the thought of being without them."

The archbishop concludes his powerful statement by advocating what he himself has done—refusing to pay 50 percent of one's federal taxes as a protest against "nuclear murder and suicide." He is convinced that "our paralyzed political system needs that catalyst. . . ." Finally he lashes out angrily at the government because "it concentrates its efforts on shipping arms to countries which need food" and because "it accords the military an open checkbook while claiming that the assistance to the poor must be slashed in the name of balancing the budget'' and because ''it devotes most of its time and energy and money to developing war strategy and not peace strategy.''

In balancing the risks involved in unilateral disarmament the archbishop appears to come out against the ''toleration'' of the possession of nuclear arms as the lesser of two evils. He thinks the possession of these lethal weapons to be an evil greater than ''constant nuclear escalation.'' The adverse reaction in Seattle and elsewhere to Archbishop Hunthausen's approach is an indication of the depths of the fears in the psyche of countless Americans and also of their self-interest, since, as the archbishop put it in his statement, ''our economic policies towards other countries require nuclear weapons.''

The restiveness among American bishops in 1981 led, as has been noted, to the appointment of a committee chaired by Archbishop Bernardin with members that included Thomas Gumbleton, president of Pax Christi USA, Bishop John O'Connor, vicar-general of the Military Ordinariate, and Bishops George Fulcher of Columbus, Ohio and Daniel Reilly of Norwich, Connecticut. The Conference of Major Superiors of Men and the Leadership Conference of Women Religious were invited to appoint representatives as consultants to the committee. Father J. Bryan Hehir, director of the USCC Office of International Justice and Peace, was staff. The committee held fourteen meetings and received the views of a wide variety of witnesses.

The seventy-five-page report of the Bernardin committee is possibly the most complete review of the moral problems of nuclear war ever issued by a Catholic body. It reiterates Vatican II by outlawing all use of nuclear weapons on civilian targets, prohibiting any threatened use, and prohibiting the first use. It allows the use of a nuclear weapon only in retaliation for a nuclear attack and then ''only in an extremely limited, discriminating manner against military targets.''

The sophisticated and nuanced proposed pastoral seeks to appreciate to the utmost the horrors of nuclear war and confesses that ''continued reliance on nuclear weapons is fundamentally abhorrent.'' The pastoral does not ''demand unilateral nuclear disarmament by the United States or its allies,'' but the use of nuclear weapons against an assault brought by conventional warfare is forbidden, since ''non-nuclear attacks by another state must be deterred by other than nuclear means.'' The pastoral repeats the 1976 message of the bishops that not only is it wrong to attack civilian populations, but it is also wrong to threaten to attack them as part of a strategy of deterrence. Indeed the *only* use permitted is the possibility of employing a nuclear weapon— presumably a tactical one—on a retaliatory basis against a specific military target. This one exception has been the most severely criticized recommendation of the pastoral. Most of the critics feel that such a situation could hardly arise and that if it did a conventional weapon would suffice.

The pastoral concedes that if this one exception were not permitted and that if every conceivable use of nuclear weapons were rejected, ''we would face the very difficult question whether it is permissible ever to continue to possess nuclear weapons.'' The pastoral weighs the arguments for and against possession: ''Abandonment of nuclear deterrence might invite an attack on the United States . . . other people deny that nuclear deterrence is in fact needed . . . perhaps . . . elimination of our nuclear weapons might, by eliminating what other countries perceived as a threat, actually contribute to, and help point the way towards, more constructive means of achieving security.''

The pastoral concludes that these positions ''are not subject to positive proof'' and that, therefore, ''we cannot lightly demand abandonment of possession of all nuclear weapons at this moment.'' A ''temporary toleration'' is permitted. *Toleration,* a technical term in Catholic theology, was used prominently in the pre–Vatican II era when the official Catholic position was that in a nation overwhelmingly Catholic the presence of non-Catholic religious bodies could be ''tolerated.'' Toleration of the possession of nuclear weapons, the pastoral insists, is not ''a comforting moral judgment'' but ''an urgent call to efforts to change the present relationship among nuclear powers.''

The pastoral openly admits that its acceptance of "toleration" will be controversial:

> Some will find toleration of the deterrent too much of a concession; they will urge a posture of disengagement and vigorous protest. Others will find toleration as far as they can go. We do not think the facts are so clear, or the moral imperative so compelling, that we can advance a judgment that is more stringent than toleration of the deterrent. But our toleration must be conditional upon sincere, substantial efforts to modify current policy as well as ultimately to eliminate these weapons.

The difficulty, of course, is that the norms for improvement are so unclear that "toleration" might continue indefinitely. If the "sincere, substantial efforts" are not successful, is there a moment in time when the nuclear escalation is so dangerous that the "temporary toleration" of the possession of nuclear arms is no longer justifiable?

The pastoral stresses repeatedly its urgent call for reduction in arms and powerfully outlines the need to give economic assistance to the Third World in order to decrease injustice and thereby to promote international stability. The episcopal letter also contains thoughtful suggestions to bring about peace, including a very firm approval of "non-violent resistance," which "deserves a serious place in any positive theology of peace."

The authors of the pastoral make note of the Catholic critics of the bishops' approach and state, without naming William Buckley or Michael Novak, that "some people who have entered the public debate on nuclear warfare . . . appear not to understand or accept some of the clear teaching of the Church as contained in papal and conciliar documents."

The pastoral expressly repudiates the position of the twelve Catholic bishops of Texas by affirming that "we cannot at this time require Catholics who manufacture nuclear weapons, sincerely believing they are enhancing a deterrent capability and reducing the likelihood of war, to leave such employment." But the document is silent about Archbishop Hunthausen's counsel to withold taxes in order to avoid complicity in the nuclear war machine.

Reaction to the pastoral is hard to evaluate, since the document was never officially released and was subsequently withdrawn. But the reactions that the pastoral itself predicted were forthcoming. The sharpest criticism came from Archbishop Philip Hannan of New Orleans, who felt that the possession of nuclear weapons should be "morally acceptable" rather than merely tolerated. Bishop Gumbleton in an interview in the *National Catholic Reporter* on July 30, 1982, admitted that he, as an acknowledged nuclear pacifist, would have preferred a stronger statement but, he felt, this will not happen "until we get to the point where we rule out the possibility of a just-war theology."

The August 13, 1982 issue of *Commonweal* magazine features the comments of nine Catholics on the draft pastoral. They seem to agree that the statement hovered between nuclear pacifism and a restatement of the just-war theory for a nuclear age. There was general approval of the utopian yearnings of the message but serious reservations about its pragmatic compromises. Sister Joan Chittister, past president of the Leadership Conference of Women Religious, calls the document "morally schizophrenic." It "steps tentatively between prophetism and nationalism." The position she desires is clear: "Let them say a clear no to nuclear war and the possession and manufacture of nuclear weapons as well."

In an unusual and unique comment, Sister Joan claims that the bishops' failure to be "morally absolute in their repudiation of the manufacture or use of nuclear weapons" undermines their credibility on the abortion issue. Her words are worth noting.

> It is troublesome to note that the bishops show no such hesitation or ambivalence about abortion. In that case from a given principle they draw universal and absolute implications with ease. Catholic hospitals may not permit abortions; Catholic doctors may not perform them; Catholic nurses may not

assist at them; Catholic monies may not be used to sponsor abortion clinics. Nevertheless, the arguments for abortion are the same: the promotion of a greater good and the deterrence of evil for the parents or a handicapped child itself, for instance. What is a woman to think? That when life is in the hands of a woman, then to destroy it is always morally wrong, never to be condoned, always a grave and unusual evil? But when life is in the hands of men, millions of lives at one time, all life at one time, then destruction can be theologized and some people's needs and lives can be made more important than other people's needs and lives? It is a theological imperative that we confront this dichotomy.

James Finn, a noted writer on peace issues, praises the bishops because "after more than three decades of the nuclear era, during which time there has accumulated a vast literature almost totally unmarked by contributions from American bishops," the bishops have taken up the responsibility that is theirs in a nation that is "the principal shaper of Western strategic policies." But Mr. Finn finds some of the moral agruments used by the bishops to be "murky." He seems to prefer a statement from the Holy See made on June 11, 1982, to be more acceptable. It was sent as a message by Pope John Paul II to the UN disarmament session: "In current conditions 'deterrence' based on balance, certainly not as an end in itself but as a step in the way towards progressive disarmament, may still be judged morally acceptable. Nonetheless in order to ensure peace it is indispensable not to be satisfied with this minimum, which is always susceptible to the real danger of explosion."

Gordon C. Zahn, a veteran peace activist who was a conscientious objector during World War II, sees in the pastoral a "troubled ambivalence and a yearning for a compromise on essentially irreconcilable issues." He fears that the document will fail to inspire and that "even the slightest indication of willingness to condone the possession and production of weapons that are admittedly immoral to use or even to threaten to use can only undermine the credibility of the entire document."

Father Charles Curran, professor of moral theology at Catholic University, perceptively points out the ambiguity in the nature of the evil that the pastoral "tolerates." Is the evil that is tolerated the intention to threaten population centers? If so, is this different from the concept of toleration as used by Catholic moral theologians in the past? If the evil to be tolerated is one's own evil intention, then there is "a new proposal in Catholic ethical thought." If, on the other hand, the evil that is tolerated is the possession of those weapons, there is a question whether the possession, absent an intention to use them, will really deter. Father Curran avers to the point mentioned by Father McCormick in the article referred to above where he states that the distinctions between possession and use "are regarded as quaint by policymakers." Policymakers who possess weapons intend to use them. Consequently, "there is no such thing, at the present time and realistically, as having nuclear weapons with no intention to use them." As a result, Father McCormick concludes, "it is this that makes the case against mere possession of such weapons so powerful."

Only one of the commentators in *Commonweal* feels that the pastoral distorts reality. "The letter misrepresents the mainline of American nuclear strategy," says Philip Odeen, a former assistant secretary of defense and a professional defense planner. Mr. Odeen asserts that "the focus of our strategy and targeting is Soviet military power not Soviet population." As a result, he feels that the pastoral accepts a "caricature of mutual assured destruction," followed in the United States, he suggests, by "a small minority on the right pushing 'war-winning' approaches. . . ."

Most of the comments in *Commonweal* and elsewhere generally credit the pastoral with coming up with the least unsatisfactory treatment possible of an intractable topic. But no one is very certain what the next steps are or where the bishops go from here.

Clearly, the entire worldwide Church is watching to see what America's bishops will do. This is particularly true for the Catholic bishops within the NATO Alliance, where their flocks are protected by the nuclear umbrella.

The opinions of these bishops are summarized in a fascinating article in the September 1982 issue of *Theological Studies* by Francis X. Winters, S.J., an articulate writer on nuclear issues and a professor of moral theology at Georgetown University. The Canadian bishops are the most militant nuclear pacifists in the West. In a statement in February 1982 they "advocated the dismantling of nuclear weapons installations in Canada, the discontinuation of Canadian manufacture of component parts of nuclear weapons," and a reexamination of Canada's role in NATO.

England's hierarchy, however, has not advanced beyond what Vatican II said about nuclear war—although Cardinal Basil Hume of Westminster has given eloquent leadership to the issue, as has Anglican Archbishop Robert Runcie. But they neither counsel unilateral nuclear disarmament nor condemn the possession of the bomb. The bishops of Scotland appear firmer than their English counterparts in condemning all use of the nuclear weapon and protest the fact that the momentous decisions about retaliation are left exclusively to government officials.

A statement in June 1982 made jointly by the French and German hierarchies speaks copiously about any alteration in the policies on nuclear deterrence. Ironically, it was members of the French hierarchy more than any other group that urged nuclear pacifism at Vatican II. These efforts to bring the Church to a radical stand were countered by some American bishops—a group that now, after the Canadians, may be the strongest antinuclear critics in the Catholic world.

Neither the Dutch nor Belgian hierarchies have spoken about the morality of nuclear deterrence. The Belgian Bishops Conference issued a statement in 1978 summarizing previous papal and conciliar pronouncements on the topic. Both this group and the bishops of the Netherlands are preparing new statements, but it does not seem likely that either group will advance beyond Vatican II.

Father Winters concludes his excellent survey by reminding us that "the urgency to pass judgment on the doctrine of assured destruction weighs more heavily on the American church than on any other." The reasons for this are clear—the Americans are the only ones that ever used the nuclear weapon and they are the principals in keeping nuclear threats credible.

In November 1982, the Catholic bishops discussed a second draft of their proposed pastoral on the moral aspects of nuclear warfare. Critical comments on the first draft from both the "hawks" and "doves" did little to alter the basic approach of the pastoral. Dropped, however, was the passage that conceded the possibility of a morally permissible attack by a nuclear weapon on a first-strike basis against a military installation. The language about deterrence and the possession of the nuclear bomb being the lesser of two evils was also eliminated. The language about "toleration" of the possession of nuclear weapons was altered. But the general thrust of the overall approach was not changed in any significant way. The twenty-five-thousand-word pastoral was, however, perceived by many to be strengthened or, at least, made more specific. Indeed, it was so specific that the White House sent a seven-page letter of protest to each of the bishops. What appeared to annoy the Reagan Administration the most was the failure of the bishops' statement even to mention the President's program for arms reduction— START. The White House letter authored by William Clark, a Catholic who is national security advisor to the President, insisted that the bishops misunderstood the Reagan approach to arms control.

The bishops forthrightly stood their ground against the contentions of the White House. The exchange of views could not be described exactly as a confrontation, but widespread comments throughout the nation showed that the position of the Catholic bishops was perceived to be a challenge to one of the fundamental premises of U.S. Foreign Policy since the early 1950's—the reliance on nuclear weapons as an essential component of America's military strategy.

Final approval of the bishops' statement, the text of which appeared in the *National Catholic Reporter* for November 5, 1982, is scheduled for May 1983. Some refinements on the statement may be made by that time, but the essential thrust of it will remain basically unchanged. That thrust is not essentially different from the position of America's Protestant churches or of other church-related bodies around the world. (The major statements made by religious groups on nuclear warfare are gathered together in the 1982 volume edited by Robert Heyer entitled *Nuclear Disarmament—Key Statements of Popes, Bishops, Councils and Churches.*)

Comments in large part critical of the draft pastoral of the American bishops will continue to appear. In *Theological Studies* for December 1982, David Hollenbach, S.J., a moral theologian, offers arguments on behalf of the case against the morality of possession for the sake of deterrence. More and more the Catholic bishops will feel required to follow the path of either the nuclear pacifists Pax Christi, to which a minority of them belong, or the position that possession for the sake of deterrence can be "tolerated." There will, of course, be the tendency and the temptation to forget about the agonizing questions involved in the nuclear issue. And this course may be possible depending upon events and developments. But if the nuclear freeze movement continues in some altered form, and if the scientists, the physicians, and the lawyers continue to command public attention, the Catholic bishops will not be able to lapse into silence or to simply reissue previous proclamations.

Is it entirely fanciful to hope and pray that in God's providence the Catholic bishops in America may provide the moral and metaphysical framework by which the United States could extricate itself from the moral morass that it has created for itself? Can we dare to hope that the bishops, relying on a well-developed Catholic doctrine on the morality of war, might join an alliance with most religious groups in the nation and bring forth a consensus that would allow America to end the nuclear age, which it alone created?

This is a fanciful hope, of course, in the sense that the elements of that consensus have yet not been identified. That consensus must bring together a new hope and a deeper faith that can overcome the fear that for almost forty years Americans have had of the Soviets and the communists. That fear is profound, pervasive, and perhaps paranoid.

ten

The Urgency of Understanding the Russians

The differences between the United States and Soviet Union are very recent indeed as history records animosities between nations. The antagonism is not something that goes back for centuries or even generations. It is not based on hostilities derived from fears of a repetition of an invasion of each other's land mass; this has never occurred. The adversary relationship, furthermore, did not even exist during World War II, when the two nations engaged in close collaboration.

The hostility is based on what some Americans would perceive as a Soviet desire to dominate the world. Ever since the fall of Peking in 1949 and the conversion by the Kremlin of Eastern Europe into "captive nations," Americans have been psychologically conditioned to think that the USSR would capture all of Europe and the United States too if only it were permitted to do so. Any public official who questions this assumption is scoffed at as "soft on communism" or treated as naive and unrealistic.

Those who think the worst about the Soviets have held an undeviating command over the mind of Americans since the dawn of the cold war. They have been able to command for the Pentagon all of the resources their worst fears tell them are necessary. The only exception to this sway over the American mind by the anti-Soviets was the Vietnam experience. But it may be that the humiliation felt by America over the fall of Saigon may be so strongly felt that it is now contributing to the syndrome that says that the United States must be strong and relentless because the Soviet Union will move into any situation where the United States is perceived to be weak or irresolute. The fear that the communists might do in Central America what they did in Southeast Asia, for instance, has resulted in the support of the Congress for an American war by proxy and through surrogates on behalf of a corrupt and authoritarian military regime in El Salvador.

Clearly, there will be increases in conventional and nuclear arms in the United States until there is a change in that deep-seated suspicion and fear of the Soviet Union that has been ingrained in the American people for almost forty years. One can compare this fear with the antagonism of the 120 million Arabs in Middle Eastern countries to the presence and the people of Israel; any objective view would have to say that the antagonism of the Arab countries is ill founded and irrational. Can it be eliminated or eroded? Not unless there exists a constant, long-term program to change the minds of Arabs—especially those who are young. In the absence of such a movement the likelihood of a change in the unbelievably strong Arab hatred of Israel will go on.

The fear and suspicion of many Americans for the government of the Soviet Union will likewise continue unless there are forces that on a long-range basis point out that the Russians are just as rational as Americans, that they are just as horrified as are people in the United States at the possibility of their cities being destroyed, and that their invasions of Eastern Europe and Afghanistan, while reprehensible, must be evaluated in comparison with what the United States tried to do in South Vietnam, what it did in Chile by destabilizing the government of Allende, and what it continues to do in El Salvador, where in 1982 it spent over $100 million in conducting a war against insurgents who want basic economic reform. Such forces do exist but are not obvious. Even the churches in America, while mandated to preach brotherly love even to one's enemies, have generally not opposed those who urge that the United States must have every conceivable weapon available for use against our "enemy." Indeed, some of the evangelicals and the Moral Majority in the early 1980s used the language of the Bible and of religion to describe the communists as "antichrist."

Since the ascendancy of Castro in 1959 the United States has dramatized its fear of communism by treating Cuba like a pariah, an enemy. What would have happened if the United States, instead of ostracizing this tiny nation ninety miles from Miami, had continued normal relations and had sought to collaborate in the economic renewal of Cuba? Those who continue to think that the United States should use every diplomatic and economic method of isolating communist nations would argue that such a policy would have legitimated and encouraged communists. And this line of thinking still prevails in America. But surely one can with equal persuasion advocate the position that the United States and the world might well be better off today if the United States had treated "totalitarian" Cuba in the same way that it had treated "authoritarian" Argentina.

Even if, however, the majority would disagree with that conclusion, they must still face the awesome reality that the traditional contempt and hatred that the United States has held for the teachings of Marxism and the policies of the Kremlin have now brought about a situation where, because of the nuclear weapon, the United States and the Soviet Union are in a relationship of mutual hostages. Putting it another way, either the hostility decreases or the likelihood of mutual destruction increases. There is, in other words, an irresistible new reason to decrease the antagonism, the fear—yes, the probability—that it will lead to the destruction of America.

The predicament is so unbelievable that no analogy is very apposite. But one can think of a situation where the enmity of two persons—such as spurned lovers or betrayed friends—reaches such a pathological point that unless it is abated, it will lead to the murder of both.

The only real hope, therefore, for the lessening of the possibility of a nuclear war is for the lessening of the tensions and hostility that brought it about in the first place—the fear of communism by the American people and the fear of American imperialism by the leaders in the Kremlin. The development of détente recognized this fact. Détente produced SALT I and SALT II. But these agreements sought only to stabilize the feelings of mutual enmity and not to reduce them. The real source of conflict was not addressed; only its potentially tragic eruptions were inhibited.

Those who, like George Kennan, urge the United States to pledge never to employ nuclear weapons on a first-use basis ground their positions to some extent in their desire to diminish the enmity that is active or latent on both sides. No American president has ever pledged that he would forgo the first use of the nuclear weapon. Indeed, the whole nuclear strategy of the United States is based on the availability of nuclear weapons should conventional forces be inadequate to repel an aggressor. But absent a pledge to renounce the first-use of the nuclear weapon, can the other side ever be expected to rid itself of the suspicions and fears that have induced them to match every major improvement in the arms race?

Ultimately, does the United States have any way out of the nuclear trap except by proclaiming to the world that it will gradually but rapidly renounce the possession of nuclear weapons? Politically, such a position is almost impossible for any administration. But ultimately is there any other way? The continuation of the arms race means, for example, that the Soviet Union will develop techniques by which it can destroy U.S. military satellites in space. Since about 75 percent of all messages about nuclear warfare come to U.S. officials from these satellites, their destruction or impairment would mean substantial, even total, malfunctioning of America's system for response to a nuclear attack by the Soviets or by anyone else. To continue the present system, therefore, without any new advances means the United States must by research come up with technology that can prevent or at least deter a Soviet inteference with those satellites essential to the instantaneous communications required by those in control of America's nuclear forces on land, in the air, and under the sea.

If, as some argue, mankind has never abandoned the technology it has discovered and that therefore nuclear weapons will be fixtures forever, the only way to prevent their use is to diminish the hostilities of those who might employ them. Americans would feel secure if the Canadians possessed nuclear weapons because, despite a common border of three thousand miles, there has never been friction between these two nations. Can that sort of relationship—or something approaching it—be developed with the Soviet Union? Again the alternative to not developing such a relationship is the continuation and the exacerbation of the nuclear arms race with all the horrors, actual and potential, that that implies.

Why do Americans persistently resist this unavoidable logical position? There are many reasons. One relates to the absence of real personal knowledge—even on the part of the best informed—about America's predicament in the arms race. Americans have been inhibited from pursuing real knowledge in the field because of the arcane terminology used. Frustration at the inability to learn about nuclear weapons has been softened by the hope and trust that the United States would never actually use a nuclear weapon.

The acceptance of the impasse in the arms race between the two superpowers as inevitable and unavoidable is not a comfortable conclusion. But the apparent absence of plausible alternatives leaves those who are horrified at the nuclear arms race no place to go. That horror led in the early 1980s to the nuclear freeze movement. But the conclusions of this movement were so vague that a liberal pro-arms-control magazine like the *New Republic* rejected the nuclear freeze proposals as unsatisfactory.

The question keeps recurring, How has it happened that citizens in America have come to believe that the United States needs 30,000 nuclear weapons to deter and/or contain the onrush of communism? Even the slightest knowledge about Russia after the 1917 revolution reveals the complexity of forces in operation in the Politburo. But somehow Americans have been pursuaded to accept the one-sided, oversimplified view that the Kremlin will, as one political figure put it, enter and burglarize every hotel room that is open on the corridor. Even if one grants the presence of some truth in this homely example, the question must be faced as to how formidable the locks on the hotel doors must be before the USSR is deterred.

It is astonishing that Americans know so little about the fears and anxieties that dominate the Soviet psyche. In the late 1930s Winston Churchill characterized the Soviet Union as "a riddle wrapped in a mystery inside an enigma." Forty years later Americans and others are still baffled.

With the failure in Western Europe of the revolution that succeeded in Russia in 1917 the Soviet Union was left largely isolated in a hostile world. Deep in the memory of Russians is the fact that the United States refused even to give diplomatic recognition to their new government until 1933. Some may also recall that the United States sent a division of 6,000 troops to the Soviet Union in 1918 to help those Russians who were trying to halt the communist takeover.

In the 1920s and 1930s the fear of the USSR deepened in the West when it became clear that the communist leaders of the world's largest nation in land area were bringing about the marriage and the merger of communist revolutionary goals with the traditional concepts of Russia's national destiny. A lot of misinterpretations of what was happening in Russia penetrated deep into the soul of the West.

Russian fears of their neighbors were intensified and perhaps made permanent when the German invasion on June 22, 1941, took Stalin by surprise. The German forces advanced to the out-skirts of Moscow. The experiences of the Soviets in World War II traumatized them profoundly. They suffered the most severe losses of any nation in World War II—about 20 million dead. Their alliance with the United States and the Western allies was too brief to relieve them of the centuries-old Russian fear of invasion from the West. Their capture of the nations of Eastern Europe and about one-third of Germany betrayed both their deep insecurity and their desire to expand their hegemony over con-tiguous countries.

The continuation by the communists of the pervasive place of the military in Russian society—contrary to Marxist dogma—was another fact that alienated the West and frightened the world. The demilitarization of Soviet society now would be so far reaching in its consequences that it is almost impossible to expect or even to hope for.

If, however, there is limited comprehension by the West of the Russians' ultimate interests, the level of understanding by the Soviets of American fears and ideals is also profoundly lim-ited. They undoubtedly find it incomprehensible that Presidents Nixon, Ford, and Carter could agree to the principles underlying SALT II only to see them rejected by the Senate. Did the igno-rance of American political process contribute to the decision to invade Afghanistan at a time when it was predictable that such aggression would cool détente, kill SALT II, and even bring to the White House, by a new election, a hard-line anti-Soviet ad-ministration? Or, as some would urge, did the invasion of Af-ghanistan indicate that the Kremlin does not care about American sensibilities and that its overarching ambition is to subjugate any territory it can?

Those questions lead to the issue that is crucial to the future of the nuclear freeze movement—what does the Kremlin *really* want? That, of course, has been the question that has tortured the American mind ever since the Soviet Union in the late 1940s became the "enemy" of the United States.

Theoretically, the advocates of the nuclear freeze could hold that regardless of how rapacious one thinks the Soviets are, the freeze is still better than the alternative, which is the continued escalation of the arms race with almost inevitable catastrophes for both sides. But the sheer logic of that position breaks down for those whose deep suspicion and fear of the Soviet Union prompts them to say that the communists are so determined to conquer the world that the United States has to have superiority rather than parity in the arms race. These persons will not, however, concede that they are opposed to the freeze; they want the Jackson-Warner freeze—a halt, but only after the United States has obtained what it concedes to be total invulnerability.

The ultimate intentions of the Soviet Union cannot therefore be deemed irrelevant in the debate about the freeze. In the handbook for the freeze movement, *Nuclear War: What's in It for You?* the authors, Roger and Earl Molander, elaborate on two views of Russia. One view is expressed by George Kennan, former U.S. ambassador to the Soviet Union, in the *New Yorker* in October of 1981, where he argues that the Soviets have a narrow view of the best way to guarantee their own security and that they are "prisoners of their own past and their country's past . . . prisoners of the rigid system of power that has given them their authority. . . ." Kennan assessed the Soviets' desire to increase their influence in the Third World as similar in origin to U.S. desires to have influence there. But Kennan also recognizes that the Soviets are potentially dangerous and that they display

> . . . certain disquieting tendencies, which oblige western policy makers to exercise a sharp vigilance. . . . I believe these tendencies reflect not so much any thirst for direct aggression as an over suspiciousness, a fear of being tricked or outsmarted, an exaggerated sense of prestige, and an interpretation of Russia's defensive needs so extravagant and so far-reaching—that it becomes in itself a threat to the security of other nations.

That less-than-assuring estimate is contrasted with the unhesitating and adamant view of Norman Podhoretz, editor of *Com-*

mentary, who wrote in that magazine in 1980 that "the Soviet Union is a revolutionary state, exactly as Hitler's Germany was, in the sense that it wishes to create a new international order in which it would be the dominant power. . . . In such an order, there would be no more room for any of the freedoms we now enjoy than there is at this moment within the Soviet Union, or any of the other communist countries. . . ."

Roger and Earl Molander do not try to reconcile the sharp differences between the perceptions of many Americans with respect to the intentions of the Soviet Union. Indeed, it is because of the inability of the United States "to resolve these conflicting views that the United States has tended to pursue first one strategy" and then another. But the central question remains: Can the Soviets "be brought into a constructive partnership committed to reduce the risk of nuclear war?"

The nuclear freeze movement has tried to prescind from the divisive and ultimately unanswerable question of what the Soviets are prepared to sacrifice to attain their eventual objectives, whatever they might be. The freeze calls for a halt now to any further nuclear buildup. It advocates SALT II because the Soviets have agreed to it in writing. The freeze movement states that the only way to get rid of the alleged window of vulnerability is to obtain a verifiable agreement from the Russians to stop developing and deploying any more missiles capable of destabilizing the present strategic balance—a balance in which both sides have so many instruments of death that they dare not use even one of them.

The nuclear freeze movement seeks, therefore, to avoid taking a position on the awful problem of the ultimate intentions of the Soviets. It assumes the basic humanity of the leaders of the Soviet Union and on that basis appeals for a halt to the redundancy, the escalation, the horrors of the arms race.

At the same time, the advocates of the nuclear freeze seek to refute the idea that the Kremlin is making advances everywhere with a geopolitical momentum. The reality is that the Soviets have been unable to command loyalty or obedience in most nations where they have infiltrated. Russia's enormous setbacks during the past several years dwarf any marginal Soviet advances in certain countries.

The facts, in other words, do not support any perception of consistent Soviet advances and devastating U.S. setbacks. Under any interpretation of world history during the nuclear age, there is no evidence to suggest that there has been a sustained, persistent Soviet geopolitical momentum.

The high point of the Kremlin's influence was in 1958, when Russian influence in China and in Indonesia was significant. The Sino-Soviet split in 1960, with the spectacular defection of mainland China, resulted in the USSR and China becoming bitter enemies with apparently no chance for rapprochement.

In 1965 another major blow came to the Kremlin when Indonesia dissolved its relationship with the Soviet Union, with General Suharto breaking all ties with Russia. The USSR had poured billions of dollars into this nation in the years 1958–65, only to see Indonesia become vehemently anticommunist.

For twenty-five years the Soviets poured billions into the Middle East; the only nation that still supports Russia in that part of the world is tiny, destitute Southern Yemen.

The same situation has developed with respect to Egypt, which received $2.7 billion from Russia, but in 1972 repudiated its $5 billion debt to the USSR and expelled twenty thousand Soviet technicians.

Some ten African nations during the past thirty-five years have had some significant Soviet influence, but now Russia influences only four—Angola, Mozambique, Ethiopia, and Algeria—among fifty nations.

In Asia the story is similar. The Soviet Union donated $5 billion to India and during the years 1962–77, India was virtually an ally of the Soviet Union. That special relationship ended abruptly in 1977 with the defeat of Indira Gandhi. India, one of the founders of the nonaligned movement, has denied military-basing privileges to the Soviets and openly opposes a permanent Soviet presence in the Indian Ocean.

In Vietnam there is, at least temporarily, some Soviet influence. Five thousand Soviet technicians are in Vietnam with perhaps $800 million per year going to that country to carry out its illegal invasion of neutral Cambodia. But one can be certain that Vietnam, after struggling for a thousand years to expel the Chinese, after having fought for almost a century to win its independence from France, and after struggling for many years to defeat the United States, is not about to become a client state or a satellite of the Kremlin.

In all of Latin America, the USSR has only one nation under its control—Cuba. Cuban or communist influence is feared by the Reagan administration to be threatening Central America, but the evidence supporting such contentions is not always strong.

Even in Afghanistan resistance is vigorous to the attempt to Sovietize that backward country. The people of Afghanistan, furthermore, are fearlessly independent; they have been fighting off outsiders since Alexander the Great, Genghis Khan, and the Mongol and British Empires.

Fifteen countries in the world at one time were members of the Soviet power system but have broken away from it. The most significant of these nations are China, India, Indonesia, Egypt, and Yugoslavia. Other nations that have left the Soviet sphere are Albania, Algeria, Bangladesh, Ghana, Guinea, Iraq, Mali, Somalia, Sudan, and Yemen.

Moscow today controls about 6 percent of the population of the world and about 5.5 percent of the gross national product (apart from the USSR). But that figure has not changed since the 1950s and 1960s, when there were major defections from the hegemony of the Soviet Union.

The trend of Soviet influence has not been increasing; it has been static or even declining. Third World nations do not find a Soviet presence or a Moscow influence attractive. History suggests that they will permit such influence only if it serves their economic purposes.

Despite this objective view of Soviet influence in the world, the fact is that the attitude of Americans to the nuclear freeze is dictated by what they thought about the Soviets over the past generation. The nuclear freeze movement has to pay attention to this perception. But can the movement persuade the vast majority of the people, both those cautious about the Soviets and those more generous in their estimate of the intentions of our adversaries, that, regardless of the level of antagonism one has toward the other side, the freezing of the level of violence is beneficial to the United States and to all of mankind? That is the painfully difficult, subtly nuanced, but supremely urgent task of the nuclear freeze movement.

eleven

Can Catastrophe
Be Averted?

A look back at the chapters in this book reveals the totality of the impasse in which Americans find themselves with regard to the nuclear arms race. Unlike most of the problems facing modern man, nuclear arms appear to be a quagmire, a conundrum, a cul-de-sac, a problem without a solution.

Reviewing chronologically what the United States has done, one can find some relief in the Nuclear Test Ban Treaty of 1963. But even if that agreement had banned all testing, there would still be the potential horror of the five nations with the veto in the United Nations also having the bomb. The Nuclear Non-Proliferation Treaty of 1968 was again a step toward restricting the availability and the use of nuclear weapons, but in the nature of things it could not control or even decelerate the arms race between the United States and the Soviet Union.

The SALT agreements initiated a rational process of controlling nuclear strategic weapons by counting them and by limiting an increase in their numbers. But, as has been seen, the SALT process did not touch tactical or theater weapons, nor did it restrict Cruise missiles or other new deadly weapons of mass destruction.

As has been noted, those who sought to control the arms race by calling for a no-first-use policy in Europe failed to elicit support, since their proposal was seen by many as undermining that deterrence that has been the linchpin of America's nuclear strategy for three decades. Similarly, those who look to the law as a source of prohibition have been disappointed.

The nuclear freeze movement, seeing the total rejection of SALT II by the Reagan administration, opted to put the whole escalating arms race on hold. In 1982 the freeze was itself put on hold by the Congress.

START is even more inadequate than SALT II. Since, furthermore, START calls for approaches never previously discussed with the Soviet Union, years will be consumed before any consensus can be expected.

Is there then any solution? Must we live forever with the situation described by General Douglas MacArthur in these words: "War has become a Frankenstein to destroy both sides . . . no longer does it possess the chance of the winner of the duel . . . it contains, rather, the germs of double suicide." Is there a framework from which one can proceed to *some* type of solution? Must the United States be forever cursed with the burden of building more sophisticated weapons in order to try to prevent a nuclear attack on New York City or San Francisco from land-based missiles in Russia, sea-based missiles in Soviet submarines, or missiles from a satellite in space? Will the one-hundredth anniversary of Hiroshima in the year 2045 see the United States still tormented by possessing weapons that it does not want to use but that, nonetheless, it will never relinquish?

Can we hope that the United States and the world might set aside nuclear weapons, as it abandoned biological and chemical warfare after World War I? In the First World War germ and nerve warfare were used. Widespread revulsion at this practice led to international agreements in the 1920s to ban biological and chemical weapons in war. Those agreements were at least one of the reasons why biological and chemical weapons were not used in World War II.

The Soviets allegedly employed this type of warfare in the early 1980s in Afghanistan and Southwest Asia. As a result, the Reagan administration felt that the United States should resume the manufacture of weapons for chemical warfare—a practice abandoned by the United States in 1969. After a stormy debate the United States House of Representatives in 1982 refused, by a vote of 251 to 159, to appropriate $54 million for binary or chemical weapons. The Senate approved the appropriation by a close vote of 49 to 45. The House's position prevailed in the conference. There will be no U.S. manufacture of chemical weapons in 1983.

Could the series of events by which biological and chemical warfare were eliminated be replicated to bring about the abolition of nuclear war? Those who refuse to succumb to the fatalistic idea that nuclear weapons will be forever the curse of mankind have hope that mankind can prevent its own incineration by nuclear weapons, just as it has prevented its asphyxiation by biological and chemical poisons. It is significant that in the debate in Congress in 1982 over financing the resumption of the manufacture of biological and chemical weapons, the proponents of the $54 million in question failed to persuade the Congress that the possession of these lethal poisons was necessary as a deterrent to their use by the Soviets. The Congress seemingly concluded that deterrence in this area is not necessary or would not be effective.

A long examination of the nuclear arms race ends with a sense of total incapacity to make any decisions as to what to do about it. One is frightened to realize that hundreds of nuclear strategists behind closed doors are planning new and appalling methods of destruction. They have all of the billions of dollars they request. They are not accountable to any public body to justify the need of the weapons they develop and deploy. They are formulating in almost total secrecy the diminishing options that will be available as Americans confront the nuclear dilemma.

In 1980 Lord Solly Zuckerman, writing in the proceedings of the American Philosophical Society, described the situation graphically. The scientists and technologists have "succeeded over the years in equating, if not confusing, nuclear destructive power with military strength . . . the men in the nuclear weapons laboratory of both sides have succeeded in creating a world with an irrational foundation, on which a new set of political realities has in turn had to be built. They have become the alchemists of our times, working in secret ways which cannot be divulged, causing spells which embrace us all."

Fred Iklé, an American nuclear arms expert, echoed this sentiment in *Foreign Affairs* magazine for January 1973 with these words: "The jargon of American strategic analysis works like a narcotic. It dulls our sense of moral outrage about the tragic confrontation of nuclear arsenals, primed and constantly perfected to unlease widespread genocide. . . ."

But even if there were total openness and an abundant amount of information available, there would still exist the same awful and awesome dilemmas. There is no way to escape from the situation in which the United States finds itself if the Soviet Union continues to be perceived as a country that can be deterred from aggression only by the threat of annihilation.

Some persons, horrified both at the prospect of the arms race and at the folly of doing nothing, will agree with Dr. Jerome Wiesner's recommendation for an "open-ended unilateral moratorium." Writing in the *Bulletin of the Atomic Scientist* in September 1982, Dr. Wiesner asserts that a "moratorium is a fresh approach" and that it is "not nuclear disarmament" but a "unilateral path to a freeze." He urges President Reagan to declare a 10 percent reduction in nuclear weapons and then wait for a response from the other side. Dr. Wiesner, one of the top scientific leaders in the area of arms control for a quarter of a century, has credibility when he urges that a "unilateral moratorium is a safe way out of this dilemma" and that it is "the quickest, possibly the only, way to start down the road to disarmament."

But there is reason to think that this approach will not be followed by the Reagan administration. So the question recurs, What to do? With pain and humiliation, one has to confess that the answer to that question may be that no one really knows. Roger Molander, the founder of the Ground Zero movement, explaining the neutral attitude of that group to proposed solutions, stated in late 1982 that "it's characteristic of this problem that thoughtful people don't know the answer yet." Since this is a factual representation of the present state of things, what should "thoughtful people" do? The answer to that inquiry clearly points to topics not directly related to the conundrum of the nuclear arms race but to altering the nature and aspirations of the Soviet Union and making it less likely that communism or Marxism will become the acceptable way of life in Third World nations. To bring about changes in the Soviet approach requires long periods of time—during which new weapons systems are being developed and deployed. Assuming, therefore, that it is not now possible to reverse the arms race, is there anything else to do but to seek to modify the attitudes and the behavior of the Soviets as well as influence the developing nations against Marxism? Both tasks are formidable. Who can understand, much less modify, the thought processes of the Politburo? If the United States came forward and offered all kinds of trade and friendship to the Soviet Union, would there be a reduction in that isolation and arrogance that have characterized the conduct of that body since 1917? Since it has never really been done—even at the height of détente—no one really knows. But even for those skeptical of offering dialogue and détente to the Soviets, the fact is that there is not really any other option. Not to follow this option is to stay with the present impasse, which inevitably can only escalate to new levels of mutual terror.

To remain, moreover, with the present standoff between the Soviet Union and the United States requires Americans to accept assumptions that are questionable and even dangerous. To hold that all of the massive deterrence now possessed by America is necessary to restrain the Soviets assumes that they would, if they could, threaten American society with nuclear weapons in order to subjugate it. The imputation of such violent intentions to the Soviets is, of course, a most serious attack on the character and nature of these people. It assumes that they are barbarians with hardly a shred of humanity. It imputes to them warlike attitudes that even Hitler may not have possessed.

But—the question recurs—how brutal would the Soviets be if they were not deterred by the threat of massive retaliation? The fact is that we simply do not know because we have never given them a chance to respond to the nuclear threat. In the late 1940s the United States formed a massive military circle around the USSR—an encirclement that, in the perception of the Soviets, almost certainly looked like a strategy that could be used to attack and overrun the Soviet Union. The desire for collective strength against the united forces of NATO and the United States—which were perceived as a threat—contributed no doubt to the 1949 alliance of the Soviet Union and China.

If the United States had not encircled the Soviet Union, what would the Kremlin have done? Would it have exercised an expansionist military policy in Europe and in other continents? Or would it have become integrated economically and politically with Western Europe? Would a policy of cooperation, rather than confrontation, with the Soviet Union in the early years after World War II have produced an entirely different world? Hardliners would say that the Soviets would have done even worse things than their seizure of East Germany or their later invasions of Hungary and Czechoslovakia. But it was the United States that, at least in the eyes of the Soviet leaders, was the aggressor in the first years after World War II. It was the United States that proclaimed that it would seek a military solution to the expansionist activities of the Kremlin.

Almost forty years after the polarization of the United States and the USSR, it is very difficult to come to any valid and verifiable assessment of the intentions of the other side. Humiliated before the world and castigated by anti-Soviet rhetoric, the Kremlin must each day be divided in its own mind whether it could or should come to terms with the United States. Soviet leaders have tried détente. They have at times proposed a thaw in the cold war and have cooperated in policies aimed at détente.

But the United States, because of its own mind-set and many other factors, still cannot know what the Soviets might do if the United States disposed of its nuclear weapons. To continue to assume, however, that the Soviets would attack the United States on a first-strike basis might well constitute something of a self-fulfilling prophecy. At least the prediction or the prophecy that the Soviets would use the bomb makes that use more, rather than less, certain.

All of this is one more demonstration of the quandary in which America finds itself. Not to change the position of the United States is a guarantee that the nuclear arms race will continue and get worse. To alter or modify America's position—fixed almost forty years ago and hardened through the years—may in the eyes of some lead to a limited, temporary vulnerability. But not to take that risk—if risk it really is—is to perpetuate the undeniably mounting risk of a nuclear war, which would not be the salvation of the United States but its suicide.

Any plea to change something basic in America's approach to its nuclear arsenal and strategy must be adopted by elected and appointed officials, who, unfortunately, can be victimized by the usually severe political risks that come to those who are accused of being weak on national defense and naive with respect to the perils of communism. Hence, the more one studies the problems involved in the issue of nuclear war, the more one recognizes that only private and nonpolitical forces can extricate America from the trap in which it is involved. Those forces will have to dampen the ingrained distrust toward the communists, educate about the follies of relying on even the possession of nuclear devices, and arouse the citizens of the United States to insist on a radical turning away from the present policies that make disasters more inevitable each day. These forces may well employ knowledge developed by psychiatrists on the irrationality of those leaders who desire some political objectives so insanely that they would allow millions of their own people to be killed. Those nongovernmental forces that seek to *force* governments to choose life and not death will, in short, employ and exploit every moral, religious, psychiatric, and military reason why the detonation of even one nuclear bomb violates common sense and goes against every instinct of rationality inherent in mankind.

One has to face, therefore, the conclusion that there is no one certain resolution of the predicament. No resolution, that is, except a change of attitudes on both sides. If the Soviet Union had the attitude of Canada toward America, both sides could destroy all their nuclear weapons immediately. Even if, however, the distrust of the USSR for the United States dissolved, the argument would be made that the United States should retain all of its nuclear weaponry and strategy lest the hostility of the Soviet Union show up in another nation. Anti-American activities and/or the expansionist tendencies of the USSR will predictably reappear in one or more nations. Consequently, the United States may well retain forever all of the labyrinthine nuclear apparatus that it has built up since 1945. Everything suggests that the United States will never become a nonnuclear power.

What then are some of the scenarios that might be expected? Let us develop a few of them.

1 / THE STATUS QUO CONTINUES

The coexistence in terror could continue for a long time. Those who proclaim the virtues of nuclear deterrence would claim that they have been vindicated. The argument would be made that the threat of massive destruction is effectual in inhibiting the Soviet Union from being more aggressive than it would otherwise be. The absence of a world conflict would produce a climate that would permit nuclear scientists and technicians to develop new methods of delivering nuclear destruction. They would develop laser technology and space satellites that would make ICBMs and even Cruise missiles far less useful than the new devices. As usual in the arms race, the scientists would leave the politicians and the moral theologians far behind.

If peace between the superpowers continues in the nuclear era, the scientists and, indeed, the arms controllers will continue to stress the necessity of stabilizing the present balance rather than reducing the number of weapons. They will urge the retention of the present system and reject any substantial change as destabilizing. One is reminded of Alexander Pope's *Essay on Man:*

> Vice is a monster of so frightful mien,
> As to be hated, needs to be seen;
> Yet seen too oft, familiar with her face,
> We first endure, then pity, then embrace.

Those who want to feel comfortable in the present nuclear standoff will be more and more aggressively advocating this scenario against those who are prophesying doomsday and an inevitable holocaust. Can the proponents of a nuclear freeze come forward with a reasoned set of scientific and social principles that will undermine the confident predictions of those who say that the nuclear arms race, while dangerous, should not be discarded because it is the only force that will continue to provide for peace between the superpowers, as it has done for over thirty years? The fact is that the advocates of the nuclear freeze tend not to enter a dialogue on this ground. They just recoil in horror and demand a halt. Such a stance allows the scientists and the nuclear strategists to continue to explain and evolve their theories of deterrence. The defenders of the status quo can tellingly point out that the proponents of the freeze have no alternative scenario that gives any hope of being attainable. The defenders of the status quo make this point forcefully in pointing out the ambiguities of Jonathan Schell's proposals in *The Fate of the Earth.* After describing apocalyptically the horrors of a nuclear war and elaborating on the dreadful dilemma confronting modern man, Schell proposes only that somehow national sovereignty be altered and that there be placed somewhere in the globe some vaguely described international body in charge of world government. Proponents of the nuclear freeze will have to do better than that.

The concept of the nuclear freeze tends to assume that it is impossible for any abiding peace to be expected or to be evolved from the existing massive accumulation of nuclear weapons. Adherents of the freeze movement would tend to agree with the Reverend Billy Graham, who in an interview in *Sojourners* magazine in 1979 spoke these words:

> The present arms race is a terrifying thing, and it is almost impossible to overestimate its potential for disaster . . . is a nuclear holocaust inevitable if the arms race is not stopped? Frankly the answer is almost certainly yes.
>
> As a Christian I take sin seriously, and the Christian should be the first to know that the human heart is deceitful and desperately wicked, as Jeremiah says. We can be capable of unspeakable horror, no matter how educated or technically sophisticated we are. Auschwitz is a compelling witness to this.

The assumption of the Reverend Billy Graham that a holocaust is almost certain may be well founded, but it has to be demonstrated to those who are afraid to break out of the contemporary situation, which, however frightening to contemplate, has not in fact resulted in war.

The rhetoric of the nuclear freeze spokesmen about the excessive expense of the nuclear arms race is open to qualification. In the fiscal year 1983 the Pentagon's budget for strategic weapons was about $23.1 billion out of $258 billion in total obligation authority. Nor can it be said with certainty that freezing or cutting back on nuclear weapons would decrease the total military budget of the United States. As has been seen, substantial financial increases for conventional weapons for NATO would be necessary if the United States renounced the first use of nuclear warheads in Europe.

Can the nuclear freeze movement maintain its mystique if it concedes that it should dialogue with arms planners, whose job it is to maintain that concept of mutual assured destruction that has been the basic U.S. foreign policy for some thirty years? Or must the nuclear freeze movement declare deterrence anathema? Up until the present time the nuclear freeze movement has been able to pass over that question by insisting that its message is simple—freeze the arms race in a mutual and verifiable way just as it stands today. Even if the professionals in the arms-control community deem this position to be simplistic, it may be that the freeze movement will have to continue its present thrust almost untouched by the arguments and the assumptions of those who deal on a daily basis with the web of fears, fantasies, and realities that make up U.S. foreign policy. Those who welcomed the nuclear freeze movement have for some time felt left out or locked out of the debate on America's nuclear policies. They got lost in the rarefied intricacies of SALT I and the even more arcane provisions of SALT II. They agree with everyone who describes the arms race as absurd, hysterical, suicidal, insane, and immoral. It is therefore not easy for them to dialogue with those who feel that mutual assured destruction is a plausible development in U.S. foreign policy and that it should be retained.

It may be that psychologically, if not logically, it is impossible for the partisans of the nuclear freeze to agree to a dialogue in which the parties assume that possibly the continuation of the coexistence in terror is the only viable option available to the United States. But if the advocates of the freeze do conclude that they find it futile to dialogue about SALT II and START, they will realize that they are outside of the "only game in town" and that they can exercise a prophetic but not a political role. Individuals can function in both roles, but a mass movement will almost inevitably have to choose a role that is either prophetic or political. If the freeze movement decides upon the prophetic role, there will be many who participate in it who will often feel themselves to be marginalized and sidelined spectators rather than players.

The millions of Americans who are desperate about the possession by their country of some 30,000 nuclear warheads are not certain where to expend their energies. They responded to the nuclear freeze movement because they understood it. They reacted favorably to the nuclear freeze movement in the ten states that had it on the ballot in late 1982. But they are at the present time undecided where to go or what to do about their inability to acquire inner tranquility as long as their country expressly and, indeed, increasingly relies on nuclear weapons as an intrinsic component of its defense posture.

The millions of Americans who are ashamed and frightened of their nation's policies on nuclear weapons constitute a potential political force of very significant proportions. If they chose to become politically active, their efforts could produce a scenario with startling consequences. Let us look at it.

2 / CONGRESS DEFUNDS ALL NUCLEAR WEAPONS

If the opponents of nuclear weapons in the United States orchestrated their efforts, could they elect a Congress with a majority of nuclear pacifists? Could one of the major political parties do what the Labour party in England did—adopt unilateral nuclear disarmament as its official policy?

The people of America elected a Congress that terminated the war in Vietnam by defunding it. Could a Congress be elected that would pass a law that simply forbade the president and the Pentagon from spending even one dollar on nuclear weapons? Such a law would make it illegal and impossible for the commander in chief to spend anything on the maintenance, development, or deployment of nuclear weapons. The scenario is highly dramatic. But it could happen. It would mean that the Pentagon would have to dismantle every nuclear device in use, since it would be illegal to spend any amount of money to maintain it. The Strategic Air Command (SAC) might have to be dissolved. Submarines with nuclear weapons would have to return these weapons to a central depository for storage or destruction. France and Great Britain could maintain their nuclear weapons in NATO, but the United States would withdraw all its nuclear weapons, both strategic and tactical. The nuclear age would end for the United States by a vote of Congress. It would no doubt be a two-thirds vote of both houses of Congress, since the president would have vetoed the comprehensive ban-the-bomb bill.

Even the most ardent opponents of nuclear war are probably not certain that they would want this particular scenario to unfold. It might expose the United States to its enemies. It would rupture American ties with its allies and, clearly, it would shatter the image of the United States as the most powerful nation in the world. The fact is, however, that the Constitution provides for precisely such a scenario and that, contrary to almost every prediction before the fact, such a scenario was played out when the American people became angry enough about America's participation in the war in Vietnam. Some may argue—and their number may be increasing—that the United States betrayed our friends when it allowed Saigon to fall and the communists to increase their influence in Southeast Asia. But the country and the Congress handled Vietnam in the way the founding fathers intended: the people of America, not the government and the military, decided what policies their nation would pursue.

Should the nuclear freeze movement—or a part of it—seek to go the political route and elect a Congress that will dramatically end American participation in the nuclear nightmare? Many will argue that it is the only way. They will point to the fact that after thousands of negotiating sessions between the superpowers over a period of twenty years, not a single nuclear weapon has been destroyed. They will argue that the rationality and basic reasonableness of the Russian people will also somehow induce or compel the leaders of the Soviet Union to follow the renunciation of nuclear war demanded by the people of America.

The deepening opposition of all of the major groups in America to nuclear war will certainly strengthen the convictions of those who want to take a bold step to end what they conceive to be nuclear madness. Their pent-up anger was expressed by Thomas Merton, the Trappist monk, some years ago: "There are activities which . . . are so dangerous and absurd as to be morally intolerable. If we cooperate in these activities we share in the guilt they incur before God. It is no longer reasonable or right to leave decisions to a largely anonymous power elite that is driving us all, in our passivity, towards ruin."

The vigor with which the Pentagon and the Reagan administration battle the nuclear freeze movement suggests that they understand and fear the way in which the logic of the freeze movement might develop. It is ultimately a movement that is probably antinuclear to the point that it is oriented toward nuclear pacifism. It does not conceal this probability but seeks to engage in the debate at a different level. Whether that level will continue to be fruitful is uncertain. But what is certain is that the nuclear freeze movement can force candidates for the presidency during 1984 to respond very clearly and specifically as to what they would do, if they were president, about the nuclear arms race. The citizens of states from New Hampshire to California are already being trained concerning questions on nuclear war that they will pose to the candidates in 1984. They will seek to make sure that the candidates will be responsive to what the American people feel and fear about nuclear war.

A Louis Harris poll taken in June 1982 revealed what Mr. Harris described as an unprecedented ''urgent hunger for peace.'' The findings are almost amazing:

1. A majority of 73 to 23 percent wants every country that has nuclear weapons to ban their production, storage, and use.

2. An even larger majority (81 to 16 percent) wants the United States and the Soviet Union to agree not to produce any more nuclear weapons, provided that there is substantial parity.

3. A striking majority (66 to 31 percent) feel that it is immoral for any country to produce more nuclear weapons.

4. By 74 to 22 percent the American people want all countries that have nuclear weapons to destroy them!

In the same poll, however, a large majority (84 percent) saw the Soviet Union as a threat to the security of the United States, and 63 percent felt that there is a likelihood over the next forty years that the Soviet Union will attack the United States. Sixty-nine percent think the Soviet leaders would use nuclear weapons if they were desperate enough.

The animosity toward Russia is not, Mr. Harris points out, due entirely to the fact that it is a communist nation, since 70 percent of all Americans now feel that China is a friend and not a hostile power. Again, the people of America have hostile feelings to noncommunist nations. Iran is viewed as hostile by 80 to 16 percent, Libya by 62 and 22 percent, and the Palestinian Liberation Organization (PLO) by 73 to 15 percent.

Summarizing the implications of these figures on the nuclear freeze movement, Mr. Harris, in an interview in the *Bulletin of the Atomic Scientist* for August–September 1982, concludes that the unique strength of the freeze movement is that it affects everyone equally. It is, he says, an issue that has aroused the common concern of people who may agree about little else. The freeze movement "cuts right across the spectrum of social and political divisions in this country. It's an idea that will not go away. It's going to be with us until the final weapons are obliterated."

3 / THE SOVIETS RENOUNCE NUCLEAR WAR

A third scenario that foresees nuclear disarmament by the Soviet Union may seem implausible. But, again, it is not impossible. The financing of a military machine with 4 million persons under arms is a severe burden on the budget and the economy of the Soviet Union. If it comes to the point that the Kremlin, simply in order to stay in office, must produce more food and consumer goods for the people, would it sacrifice some part of the military and would that part be its nuclear weaponry? It might well be that new U.S. developments such as the Cruise missile will cost the Kremlin billions of dollars just to catch up. Would a pragmatic, political decision be reached to forgo nuclear weapons? It could be announced to the world with a huge propaganda campaign designed to portray the Soviet Union as the foremost peace-making nation in the world. Or, alternatively or simultaneously, could the Russian people develop their own nuclear freeze movement and insist that their government give them bread and not bombs?

Are there ways by which developments of this kind can be encouraged within the Soviet Union? Theoretically, the Voice of America has been doing precisely that for a generation. It may be that the citizens of Russia, hearing about the freeze movement in America, would be inspired to make known their own feelings about the bomb to their leaders.

Could it come about that the highest elected leaders of the United States, fearful that the Congress was about to defund America's nuclear arsenal, would move toward a mutual nuclear disarmament with the Soviet Union? That is what happened, it will be recalled, with the ABM. President Nixon knew that the chances of getting the Congress to fund the ABM were problematical at best. The reluctance of the Congress to finance the ABM was due in large part to the widespread agitation by millions of people who did not want the ABM in their community. Could a similar scenario evolve by which the superpowers would reach a bilateral agreement to drop nuclear armaments? Assuming the inherent rationality of both sides, nuclear disarmament by mutual consent is not only possible but probable.

Russia in the post-Brezhnev era may be a very different place than it has been since it assumed hegemony over Eastern Europe after World War II. That domination could fade away. A successful rebellion by one of the satellites might bring freedom to all of them. They could move ideologically and culturally toward Europe and the West—further isolating the Soviet Union. The diverse ethnic groups, moreover, within the USSR could also insist upon their autonomy and their freedom. The Soviet Union in fact might even lose the status of a superpower. An accumulation of economic problems could, furthermore, force it to set aside whatever aspirations it had for global domination.

The present nuclear policy of the United States seems to assume that Russia will always be its relentless, aggressive self. While it is not appropriate to rely on great and beneficial changes after the passing of Brezhnev, it is appropriate to think that such changes might occur—especially if the United States works for them. The possibilities of greater friendship with the Soviet Union in the post-Brezhnev period are not enhanced by a massive program to surround the USSR with Cruise missiles. Nor is friendship developed by denying the Soviets the advantages of American technology to build a pipeline for natural gas from Siberia to Europe.

The advocates of the nuclear freeze might well assist in the birth of a new relationship between the USSR and the United States if they made an issue of including Cruise missiles in negotiations at the disarmament talks in Geneva. The Cruise missile represents a new watershed in the arms race. As noted above, it is a precision-guided drone that can skim hundreds of miles at treetop level and deliver a nuclear warhead with great accuracy. President Reagan's START proposal says nothing at all about Cruise missiles. In September 1982 in an interview in the *New York Times,* Major General Viktor Starodubov of the Soviet General Staff made it clear that the principal Soviet aim at Geneva is to slow or stop the development of American Cruise missiles. The United States is focusing on land-based missiles, in which the Soviets have invested extensively. The United States fears the "heavy" ICBMs of the Soviets as a special threat because they are fast, accurate, and carry large numbers of warheads.

The Pentagon has made it clear throughout the SALT and START talks that it has no intention of giving up its Cruise missiles. They expect to have them available to all units of the triad by 1984. Could not the freeze movement turn public attention to the Cruise missile and insist that the United States halt its production and deployment? It will possibly be a no-win fight, since the Cruise missile is a very attractive weapon to the military. But if the Soviets thought that there was some chance of the United States dropping the Cruise missile, it might be amenable to giving up some of its land-based ICBMs. In any event, the nuclear freeze movement has to concentrate not only on the buildup of arms in the United States but must develop a strategy that, like the controversies over radioactive testing in the atmosphere and the ABM, could lead to agreements by the superpowers.

Better communications between East and West, a centerpiece of détente, was emphasized in the Helsinki agreements signed by President Ford on August 1, 1975. Under this pact thirty-three European nations, including the Holy See, agreed with the United States and Canada to maximize cultural contacts between the peoples of the signatory nations and to protect a wide variety of rights. The Helsinki nations gather together on a regular basis and talk about compliance. The meetings are never easy, but the Helsinki process is one available way by which some understanding between the NATO and Warsaw Pact nations can be sought.

Are there not countless other ways by which détente, discussion, dialogue, and debate can be increased? Searching for such ways is an essential element in the making of peace. In the post-Brezhnev era a mutual searching for peace between the superpowers could be very fruitful if the United States, the superpower that has always led in the nuclear arms race and that now leads by reason of the Cruise missile, among other things, comes forward with a plan that allows both sides to have parity. The nuclear freeze movement, rather than just calling for a cessation of development and deployment, must go beyond this negative and neutral position and advocate specific, creative, and inventive plans. It might have to work with the people, rather than the politicians, of Russia, just as it appealed to people of all kinds in the United States.

4 / A NUCLEAR CATACLYSM OCCURS

Any contemplation of the nuclear arms race often leads to the sober conclusion that mankind will almost inevitably employ the nuclear bomb again. Indeed, it seems almost like a miracle that mankind, so prone to abuse good forces for evil purposes, has not in almost forty years employed the nuclear weapon. But its use seems almost inevitable—by mistake or madness, if not by malice.

Would a cataclysm involving the death of millions of people so shock humanity that somehow legal means would be found to banish the bomb? Possibly. But its use could permit strong anticommunists to argue that, after all, "only' a small percentage of humanity was wiped out and that their deaths have enhanced human freedom.

Because this mentality exists it is useful to have films that show the irreparable damage that is done by a nuclear attack. *The Final Epidemic* is such a film. Cosponsored by a broad coalition of antinuclear groups, it reveals what would happen to San Francisco if a bomb struck. The damage is beyond imagining. One of the most gruesome consequences is that the city would be sealed off indefinitely and that it would remain forever as the cemetery for three hundred thousand corpses burned beyond recognition.

The possibility of a cataclysm will continue to radicalize people. These individuals will apply the adage of Thoreau to the situation: "There are a thousand hacking at the branches of evil to one who is striking at the root." They will quote the searing words of George Kennan, who when he resigned thirty years ago as director of the State Department Planning Office wrote the following in a letter to Secretary of State Dean Acheson: "The weapons of mass destruction . . . reach backward beyond the frontiers of Western civilization to the concepts of warfare which were once familiar to the Asiatic hordes. They cannot be reconciled with a political purpose directed to shaping, rather than destroying, the lives of the adversary. They fail to take account of the ultimate responsibility of men for one another, and even for each other's errors and mistakes. . . ."

It is not certain that a nuclear attack killing millions in the United States would bring Americans to accept nuclear pacifism. It might just so enrage and humiliate them that they would be even more belligerent than they were before the attack. This would be especially true if the United States for some reason did not retaliate against the Soviet Union. But what is certain is that a nuclear attack with even a moderate impact would slow down the progress of the nation in countless ways. Thousands of burn victims would divert massive numbers of medical personnel from their ordinary pursuits. Bombed cities would require enormous federal subsidies. Vast communications networks would need billions of dollars to be replaced. The list could go on and on. Even a minor nuclear attack could paralyze the United States for a long period of time. It would retard economic progress just like the plague in the Middle Ages that killed one-third of all persons then alive impeded human development in countless ways.

If the unthinkable happened, it might strengthen the bizarre hold that nuclear weapons have on the imagination of some persons. It might arouse vengeance. It could produce an orgy of self-pity that could find an outlet in acts that would bring further shame and degradation on those who participated in them.

5 / CIVIL DISOBEDIENCE AND NONVIOLENCE

America has always had a profound respect for civil disobedience, although it has rarely been practiced or been tolerated in the law or in the courts. "Dissent without civil disobedience is consent," said Thoreau.

Will civil disobedience over nuclear weapons grow and swell until it is a problem beyond containing or handling? It could. Civil disobedience, of course, goes beyond peaceful demonstrations. It includes violations of the law with the understanding that those who transgress the law will accept the penalty. The most obvious kind of civil disobedience would be the withholding from one's federal taxes that portion of the tax spent on nuclear weaponry. For many years there have been perhaps a few thousand who have refused to pay a very small federal excise tax levied on phone bills in order to pay for the costs of war. The government simply obtained the withheld funds by convenient and legal means. Could the anger and indignation over nuclear weapons mount up so that millions would be withholding substantial sums from their federal taxes? If the example of

Archbishop Hunthausen, mentioned above, is widely contagious, a serious problem for law enforcement officers could develop.

The nuclear freeze movement has not adverted to this technique of protest; nor is there any indication that it will. But if the freeze is frustrated over a substantial period of time, will those already in anguish over their nation's involvement with nuclear warfare turn to something more dramatic, more direct, and more dangerous? What if the same percent of taxpayers refused to pay taxes for war purposes as has refused to register for the draft— 10 to 12 percent of the total number of eighteen-year-old men? What if whole religious denominations announced a joint decision not to pay a portion of their taxes? Or what would happen if a large group of skilled technicians refused to participate any longer in making parts for nuclear weapons?

The answer to these questions will depend upon the level of guilt that the nation feels for what it did at Hiroshima and what it has done in the years since that fateful day. The freeze movement has evoked the latent guilt that countless Americans have always felt for America's role in making the nuclear age possible. That guilt could grow and deepen. Vast numbers of Americans could come to feel that it was the United States more than any other nation or force that brought the nuclear nightmare into existence. The guilt that would result from this conviction could torment individuals to the point where they will be compelled by conscience to do something extraordinary in order to expiate their guilt. It is impossible to predict what they might do, but it could be bold, brave, and, at least in some eyes, beautiful. These people have come to agree with George Kennan, who said in 1982 that "there is no issue at stake in our political relations with the Soviet Union—no hope, no fear, nothing to which we aspire, nothing we would like to avoid—which would conceivably be worth a nuclear war."

These persons also agree with Karl Barth, who in 1959 remarked that the churches' inability to take an unequivocal stand against nuclear war was their greatest theological failure since their failure to stand firmly against the emergence of Nazism in Germany.

If the guilt over nuclear war becomes acute, we might see a version of the freedom movement of the 1960s, where thousands refused to sit in the back of the bus or to be denied a seat at the white-only lunch counter.

Many churches are (perhaps inadvertently) encouraging such a movement, since they have denounced as immoral the use that the United States makes of nuclear deterrence. In September 1982 the nation's Episcopal bishops severely condemned nuclear war. In the same month the American Lutheran church, by a vote of 861 to 33, urged "the elimination of nuclear weapons from the earth." The Catholic bishops, as noted above, suggest that the possession of nuclear weapons may be "tolerated" but that such "toleration" can be morally acceptable only if there are clear signs of progress being made to extricate the nation from the possession of nuclear weapons, which, morally, may never be used.

Civil disobedience, passive resistance, and forms of nonviolence have seldom been necessary over an extended period of time in American history. Remedies for intolerable conditions have been found in the legislatures or in the courts. The struggle over slavery and the movement to obtain equality for blacks found solutions eventually in constitutional amendments and decisions of the United States Supreme Court. Neither of these remedies is available to those who decry America's threat of nuclear annihilation of the Soviets. They have to take on the Pentagon, the Congress, and the White House. If redress and relief are not found, the opponents of America's nuclear war machine may resort to a series of nonlegal solutions. They might all be predictably unsuccessful. But those who engage in them can justify their actions by claiming, quite correctly, that they saw no other solution to the nuclear impasse. They can claim that they have followed the only way made known to them by their convictions and their conscience. If they are consistently convincing, they might accomplish what Gandhi eventually achieved.

For those who have given up on a political solution and who are not religious (or who do not think that religion can or will alter the mind of a majority of Americans on the nuclear issue), civil disobedience on behalf of nuclear pacifism may well appear to be the only way to protest. If enough people come to this conclusion, the government may be induced to give up its nuclear arsenals rather than have millions of people daily defying the laws of the land.

6 / AMERICA CONTAINS COMMUNISM BY FEEDING THE HUNGRY

There is little indication that the United States will in the foreseeable future give up its foreign policy of containing communism. That objective has sunk deep into the psyche of the American people. Almost without exception, even the most radical person, young or old, will not reject outright America's commitment to prevent communist aggression. Many of those who felt that America's entrance into the war in Vietnam was a mistake will say that a land war in a faraway country where the United States takes sides in a civil war is a mistake. But few will rule out the idea that sometimes the United States should contain communism. There are not too many who would totally reject America's role in the Korean War, even though the present government in South Korea, still defended by some forty thousand American troops, is far from an ideal democracy.

The real question then is this: If a war, Vietnam-style, is not appropriate and if deterrence by nuclear threat is wrong, how is America supposed to contain communism? One of the purposes of American foreign economic aid was to attract the nations of the Third World to American ideals and to discourage them from being attracted to the Soviet sphere of influence. The troubled history of foreign aid, with its intermingling of military and economic aid, does not yield a quick answer as to whether it has in fact contained communism. But it seems clear that if the United States helped the hundred countries that have become new nations during the nuclear age, the governments and the peoples of these countries would have admiration and gratitude for the United States. Again, the record is not clear that all nations have been as grateful as America would hope. But the general principle holds that nations would be far less inclined to accept Marxism in economics or in politics if they had a constructive relationship with the United States and if they felt that the American government was not allowing American corporations to exploit them. The animosity toward America so often present in the attitude of developing countries toward multinational corporations is not necessarily going to be eliminated by additional aid from the United States. But the nations the United States really helps are more probably the friends of the United States than of the USSR.

The Reagan administration has in effect conceded this principle by making available all forms of sophisticated military hardware to Third World nations. As noted above, there has been an explosion of sales of conventional weapons in the first two years of the Reagan administration. If there were an explosion of all types of economic aid—technology, loans, agricultural counseling—would the United States be "containing" communism? The answer has to be yes. But the history of foreign aid has been so bedeviled with problems that it would be very difficult to persuade many people that the road to attracting underdeveloped nations to America's sphere of influence is to give them economic assistance.

But the truth of the familiar principle remains: countries that are troubled and torn apart by poverty, malnutrition, and illiteracy are easy prey for communist influence.

Could, therefore, a scenario develop that would have the United States containing communism by increasing its foreign economic aid? Clearly, the United States does not now seriously consider its foreign aid program as an important element in its policy of containing communism. The United States ranks fifteenth out of seventeen nations with respect to the share of its gross national product that it allocates to the Third World. Its contributions to the international lending units like the World Bank have declined steadily.

Would the United States be containing communism if it confronted the world as it is in all of its poverty and anguish and extended itself to offer relief? There will be 2 billion more human beings to care for in the next seventeen years before the dawn of the year 2000. The population of the world will increase from 4.2 to 6.2 billion.

The existing poverty of the world's children will be aggravated by this spectacular increase in global population—the greatest increase in any comparable period in human history. The 1982 UNICEF report contained these appalling facts:

1. Of the 125 million infants born in 1982, 17 million will be dead before their fifth birthday.
2. One hundred million children go to bed hungry every night.
3. Two hundred million children (one-third of them in the Third World) age six to eleven have no school to go to.
4. Five hundred thousand children a year contract polio because they do not receive vaccines.

President Carter expressed this grim reality vividly when he noted in an address in October 1977 to the United Nations that ''last year the nations of the world spent more than sixty times as much equipping each soldier as we did educating each child.''

The friends of the nuclear freeze do not reject the containment of communism as one of the goals of American policy. But their stance and approach would appear as a more positive one if they stressed that the containment of communism can be done more effectively by making people admire and respect the United States than by building nuclear arsenals. Even more importantly, the freeze should stress that if the arms race continues to grow— reaching global levels of spending for military purposes of some $700 billion in 1984—it will be literally impossible to feed the 800 million people who are chronically malnourished or to educate the growing millions of children who will be afflicted with illiteracy all of their lives. The United States and the West cannot have it both ways: if they continue their present levels of spending for military purposes, they will impoverish the Third World and thereby render the millions of persons in that part of the globe vulnerable to the blandishments of communism. The Second Vatican Council said it clearly in 1965: "While extravagant sums are being spent for the furnishing of ever new weapons, an adequate remedy cannot be provided for the multiple miseries afflicting the whole modern world."

Would Angola, Cambodia, or Cuba have resisted communism if the United States had been more generous with them before they accepted Soviet domination? No one can say for certain. But friendship and help from individuals and nations is more likely to create mutually beneficial alliances than anything else.

Other scenarios are possible. Some Idi Amin could obtain a nuclear weapon and blackmail a nation or a group of nations into submission. Or some other mad tyrant could actually detonate the bomb in one or both of the superpowers, thereby destroying entirely the present geopolitical balance of the world. Or South Africa, Israel, Taiwan, or some of the other nations thought to have the capacity to construct a nuclear bomb might do so, bringing about a whole new series of destabilizing influences across the globe.

One of the most disconcerting elements in the present nuclear situation is the certainty that there is no certainty about what the next development will be. There is no stability, despite the assurance by the nuclear strategists and the arms controllers that destabilizing developments can be predicted. The present predicament is viewed with apprehension, anxiety, and anger. These are the qualities, mingled with fear, that are at the heart and soul of the nuclear freeze movement.

What should those who dread nuclear war do next? If the followers of the freeze knew the answer to that question, they would write the script and perform it. They don't. No one does. Nothing has worked over the period of almost forty years. Can something new or old work now? One can only hope.

The lack of knowledge on how to extricate mankind from the nuclear trap is particularly painful for Catholics. Their theology on good and evil has been refined through the centuries and their moral philosophy on the nature of war is more developed than it is in many other religions. They have, in addition, a well-organized and highly centralized religious body embracing 18 percent of the world's total population with 783 million adherents, 961,000 nuns, and 413,600 priests. Is it not possible for such a group to give global guidance that would deliver humanity from the nuclear scourge?

The pain for American Catholics is particularly acute, since it was the United States that invented the nuclear age and developed nuclear weapons over a long period of time—with very little protest from America's Catholics until the late 1970s.

In the face of the enormity of evil that inheres in the nuclear menace, one hesitates to outline what individual citizens or groups might profitably do. But, clearly, all should learn and understand more about nuclear issues and should act in appropriate and useful ways.

The level of comprehension about nuclear issues is quite low in America. Persons who have read this book may have knowledge that places them in the top 1 or 2 percent of all Americans. If the nuclear freeze movement is to have a greater credibility, it must strive to bring forth persons who can speak with some authority about the complicated controversies involved in the nuclear arms race. A small coterie of professionals who have worked for many years with or for the government now dominates the arms-control dialogue—they frame the questions. Over the past four years they have forced the discussion to center on issues such as the B-1 bomber, the MX, and the alleged window of vulnerability.

Can the freeze movement train a group of well-informed spokesmen who can hold their own in a dialogue with those who have been immersed for several years in the jargon and the mystique of nuclear weapons? Theoretically, it is possible. Practically, it will be very difficult. But at least there could be developed a large group of persons who are knowledgeable enough to alter public opinion by presenting clear information and solid arguments. The number of such citizen-advocates may always be relatively few, since the issues involving the nuclear arms race are more complicated than the issues involved in the Vietnam War or the environment—areas where citizen impact was decisive.

On the other hand, persons who do not possess a mastery of the vocabulary used by the nuclear experts should not be deterred from expressing their view. They can quite plausibly assert that they have a very clear position on the morality involved even if they do not claim to know very much about nuclear physics or international diplomacy. But even so, such persons can be dismissed by the professionals as naive and simplistic. And that is precisely the approach that has been taken by the opponents of the nuclear freeze movement. These opponents will have an increasingly difficult time if those whom they stigmatize as naive can be counted in the millions, spanning every class and age in America.

Nevertheless, complete knowledge about nuclear warfare to citizen-lobbyists is essential. That knowledge is now becoming more available and more comprehensible due to organizations like the Federation of American Scientists, SANE, Physicians for Social Responsibility, Lawyers Alliance for Nuclear Arms Control, and a proliferation of similar groups.

But even if millions become informed, effective action will be required. The action can be educational, political, religious, or legal. Anything that raises the consciousness of Americans about the horrors of nuclear war is effective. But what is the action or strategy that will substantially change America's foreign policy, with its reliance on nuclear weapons? When one is talking about such a revolutionary change, one hesitates to pronounce or predict what action will bring about the change that is required. It will in all probability not be one single act or event; it will be a long series of acts bringing about perhaps imperceptibly an attitude that will finally compel America to renounce or abandon the shameful and scandalous threat that it now uses to hold all potential enemies hostage.

Action will not necessarily emerge from those who are informed about nuclear issues. As the opposition to the freeze hardens, the proponents of the freeze will be derided as unrealistic, extremist, and unpatriotic. The barrage against the freeze will silence not a few. Very soon it may be that the best and the brightest among would-be antinuclear spokesmen will be intimidated by the powerful in the Pentagon and the right-wing establishment. Those who believe in the nuclear freeze may have to be reminded that in the nuclear age, the sin of silence may be the greatest offense against God and man.

Those who will want to become informed and to be influential on nuclear issues will need information and encouragement from all types of sources. They will welcome and practically memorize moving statements like that of George Kennan, who, on the occasion of his accepting the Albert Einstein Peace Prize in 1981, reminded us of these solemn truths:

> But we must remember that it has been we Americans who, at almost every step of the road, have taken the lead in the development of this sort of weaponry. It was we who first produced and tested such a device; we who were the first to raise its destructiveness to a new level with the hydrogen bomb; we who introduced the multiple warhead; we who have declined every proposal for the renunciation of the principle of "first use"; and we alone, so help us God, who have used the weapon in anger against others, and against tens of thousands of helpless non-combatants at that.

But even compelling statements like that will not be enough. There will be a constant need for involvement in a community where one's commitment and courage are daily renewed. One needs to be reminded that the struggle is against an invisible monster described by the political and military establishment of the United States as essential to the national security of the nation and the stability of the free world. There will be the need to realize that we are now in the midst of a revolution in which the scientists, the physicians, the lawyers, and the bishops of America have declared war on the central dogma of American foreign policy—the alleged necessity of deterrence by weapons whose use is too hideous to contemplate. To persevere in the advancement of such a revolution requires a great deal of faith and vision. It will be easy to sit on the sidelines. To blindly follow the dictates of those in power will be described by countless persons and groups as the role of a proud anticommunist patriot.

One of the most perceptive analyses of the nuclear tragedy appeared in a statement issued by representatives of churches in the United States and the USSR after a consultation on disarmament in Geneva in March 1979. After denouncing the ''spiral of terror'' of the arms race, the group of two dozen churchmen from both superpowers stated that ''seeking our security through arms is in fact a false and idolatrous hope . . . true security can be found only in relationships of trust . . . these relationships we believe to be possible, for Christ has overcome the principalities and powers'' (Colossians 2:15).

If Christians in America really believe this statement, they will seek to bring about ''relationships of trust'' with the Soviet Union. That may be an enormously difficult task. But it is a task that no one may refuse or reject. That task was described by Christ in the Gospel in the unforgettable words, ''Blessed are the peacemakers; for they shall be called the children of God.''

The solution to the nuclear agony will depend upon how many people have the desire and the determination to want to be called ''the children of God.''

Bibliography

Beres, Louis Rene. *Apocalypse: Nuclear Catastrophe in World Politics.* Chicago, IL: University of Chicago Press, 1980. The impact of nuclear arms and strategic theory on international politics is analyzed in this moderately technical book.

Clarke, Duncan. *The Politics of Arms Control.* New York: Free Press, 1981. The work of The Arms Control and Disarmament Agency is reviewed.

Freedman, Lawrence. *The Evolution of Nuclear Strategy.* New York: St. Martin, 1981.

Ground Zero. *Nuclear War: What's in It for You?* New York: Pocket Books, 1982. This paperback examines the history of the arms race, the consequences of a nuclear exchange, and the future technological developments that will threaten survival.

Hatfield, Mark and Kennedy, Edward. *Freeze! How You Can Help Prevent Nuclear War.* New York: Bantam Books, 1982. Two U.S. Senators explain the freeze phenomenon, and answer questions about the freeze.

Hersey, John R. *Hiroshima.* New York: Knopf, 1946.

Heyer, Robert, ed., *Nuclear Disarmament: Key Statements of Popes, Bishops, Councils and Churches.* Ramsey, NJ: Paulist Press, 1982.

Kincaide, William H., and Porro, Jeffrey D., editors. *Negotiating Security: An Arms Control Reader.* Washington, D.C.: Carnegie Endowment for International Peace, 1979. A collection of articles from *Arms Control Today* concerning the negotiation of arms control agreements, nuclear strategy, and weapons, regional arms control and arms control institutions such as ACAD and the U.N.

Office of Technology Assessment. *The Effects of Nuclear War*. Washington, DC: U.S. Government Printing Office, 1979. An overview of the consequences of possible nuclear attacks, on both the U.S. and the U.S.S.R., by forces ranging from a single weapon to most of the existing arsenals. It addresses the short- and long-term social, economic and physical effects.

Pierre, Andrew J. *The Global Politics of Arms Sales*. Princeton, NJ: Princeton University Press, 1982. The interests of suppliers of conventional arms and the importing countries are considered in this work. The effect of arms sales on both domestic policy and regional balances is discussed.

Seaborg, Glen T., and Loeb, Benjamin S. *Kennedy, Krushchev, and the Test Ban*. Berkeley: University of California Press, 1981.

Smith, Gerard. *Doubletalk: The Story of SALT I*. Garden City, NY: Doubleday and Co., 1980. Ambassador Smith presents an insider's detailed account of the ebb and flow of the SALT I negotiations, as well as the impact of American domestic events on the negotiations.

Stanford Arms Control Group. *International Arms Control: Issues and Agreements*. Stanford: Stanford University Press, 1976.

Schell, Jonathan. *The Fate of the Earth*. New York: Knopf, 1982.

Talbott, Strobe. *Endgame: The Inside Story of SALT II*. New York: Harper & Row, 1979. A highly readable account of the persons, processes, and politics involved in the negotiation of the SALT II agreement.

U.S. Arms Control and Disarmament Agency. *Arms Control and Disarmament Agreements: Texts and History of Negotiations*—1980 Edition. Washington, DC: U.S. Government Printing Office, 1980. The texts of all major arms control and disarmament agreements in which the U.S. has been a participant since 1925, together with a short discussion of each by the staff of the U.S. Arms Control and Disarmament Agency.

Walzer, Michael. *Just and Unjust Wars*. New York: Basic Books, Inc., 1977. A moral and theoretical analysis of war, this book presents many historical examples of dilemmas confronted.

Index

A

Acheson, Dean 149
Action-reaction phenomenon
   45, 75, 97
Afghanistan 9, 56, 57, 61, 88,
   125, 129, 133
Albania 129
Algeria 128, 129
American Bar Association 73,
   95
American Legion 72
American Lutheran Church 108,
   152
American Security Council 72
Amin, Idi 156
Anglican Church 99
Angola 15, 64, 128, 156
Anti-ballistic missile (ABM)
   44–46, 59, 61, 76, 103, 146,
   148
Aquinas, Thomas 104
Argentina 15, 121
Aristotle 94
Arms Control & Disarmament
   Agency (ACDA) 9, 38, 39,
   57, 72, 94

Arms Control Association 4
Arms Control Today 17
Arms Export Control Act 10
Atomic Energy Commission,
   US 33, 41; UN 25
Atoms for Peace 36
Augustine, Saint 104
Australia 18
Ayacucho—See Declaration of
   Ayacucho

B

B-1 bomber 59, 73, 157
Backfire bombers 3, 51, 53, 77
Bangladesh 129
Barth, Karl 55, 151
Baruch, Bernard 25, 26, 28
Baruch plan 25–28, 32–34
Bernardin, Joseph 107, 109
Bikini Islands 39
Biological warfare—See Chemi-
   cal & biological warfare
Bishops, Catholic, US 2, 7,
   103, 105–107, 109, 111,
   114–17, 152; Canadian 115;

Scotland 115; French 115; German 115; Episcopal 152
Brezhnev, Leonid 51, 146–48
Britain 12–14, 18, 27, 28, 42, 80, 83, 92, 97, 142
Broomfield, William 72, 76
Brown, Harold 70
Brzezinski, Zbigniew 52, 53
Buckley, James 15
Buckley, William 111
Bundy, McGeorge 79, 81–83
Bush, George 106

C

Cambodia 129, 156
Canada 123, 138, 148
Carter, James E. 10, 18, 41, 51–53, 56–58, 61, 64, 70, 106, 125, 155
Carter administration 10, 12, 14, 15, 17, 41
Casaroli, Agostino 8
Case Against SALT II 57
Catholic Bishops—See Bishops, Catholic
Catholic Church 100, 102–107, 157
Catholic Conference, U.S. 55, 105, 107, 109
Chemical and biological warfare 7, 100, 132, 133
Chile 15, 17, 120
China—See People's Republic of China
Chittister, Joan 112
Churchill, Winston 27, 124
Civil defense 78, 107
Civil disobedience 150, 152, 153

Clark amendment 15
Clark, William 116
Clarke, Duncan 39
Cold war 5, 27, 34, 61, 120
Commentary Magazine 57, 61, 74, 126
Committee on the Present Danger 55, 57
Common Cause 66
Common Security—A Blueprint for Survival 8
Commonweal Magazine 55, 112, 114
Comprehensive Test Ban Treaty 41, 42
Conference of Mayors 66
Congressional Record 71
Congressional Research Service (CRS) 12
Conventional arms 6, 8–19, 30, 54
Cruise missiles 1, 49, 51, 53, 59, 60, 68, 71, 73, 83, 97, 99, 131, 138, 145, 147, 148
Cuba 18, 57, 121, 129, 156
Cuban missile crisis 39, 61
Curran, Charles 114
Czechoslovakia 61, 136

D

Declaration of Ayacucho 17
Dense pack 59
Detente 50, 64, 83, 122, 125, 135, 136
Deterrence 57, 79, 81, 89, 96, 106, 110, 111, 113, 116, 117, 135, 138, 139, 148, 152, 160
Dirksen, Everett 43

Dresden 23
Dulles, John Foster 34

E

Economist, The 86
Ecuador 17
Egypt 16, 128, 129
Eighteen Nation Disarmament
  Conference 39
Einstein, Albert 74, 159
Eisenhower, Dwight D. 13,
  34–37, 74
Eisenhower administration 38
El Salvador 3, 18, 120, 121
Endgame 53
Essay on Man 139
Ethiopia 64, 128
Evolution of Nuclear Strategy 3

F

Falk, Richard 89
Falkland Islands 3
Fate of the Earth, The 139
Federation of American Scien-
  tists 158
Fellowship of Reconciliation 99
Final Epidemic, The 149
Finn, James 113
"First use" 1, 79–82, 85, 87,
  88, 109, 122, 137
Ford, Gerald 51, 125, 148
Foreign Affairs 79–82, 94, 134
Foreign Affairs Committee,
  House 65, 72
Foreign Relations Committee,
  Senate 65
France 12, 13, 15, 17, 18, 29,
  40, 80, 86, 92, 129, 142
Fratricide 70

Freedman, Lawrence 3
Freeze—See Nuclear Freeze
Fulcher, George 109

G

Gaither, H. Rowan, Jr. 35
Gandhi, Indira 128
Gandhi, Mahatma 101, 152
de Gaulle, Charles 29
Gelb, Leslie 17
Geneva Conference on Disarma-
  ment 16
Geneva Convention 2, 90, 93,
  94
Genocide Convention 93, 95
Germany, East 35, 84, 136
Germany, West 12, 21, 30, 32,
  40, 44, 80, 82, 84, 86, 124,
  125, 152
Ghana 16, 129
Global Politics of Arms Control
  12
Graham, Billy 140
Gromyko, Andrei 52
Guinea 16, 129
Gumbleton, Thomas 55, 109,
  112

H

H-bomb 33, 34, 39, 60
Hague Convention 2, 90, 92, 94
Hague Rules of Land War 91
Hannan, Philip 112
Hatfield, Mark 58, 75, 76
Hehir, J. Bryan 55, 56, 109
Helsinki 148
Hersey, John 24
Heyer, Robert 117
Hitler, Adolph 27, 55, 84, 127,
  136

Hiroshima 5, 21–25, 30, 31, 42,
43, 45, 54, 67, 78, 90, 91,
95, 100, 103, 132, 151
Hiroshima, novel 24
Hollenbach, David 117
Hoover, Herbert 26
Hume, Basil 115
Humphrey, Hubert 38
Hungary 35, 61, 136
Hunthausen, Raymond 108,
109, 111, 150

I

ICBM 1, 3, 35, 44, 53, 54, 60,
68–70, 77, 138, 147
Ikle, Fred 94, 134
India 9, 29, 92, 128, 129
Indonesia 16, 128, 129
International Arms Control 44
International Atomic Energy
Agency 36
International Independent Com-
mission on Disarmament and
Security Issues 25
Iran 3, 14, 57, 145
Iraq 3, 14, 18, 129
Israel 18, 120, 156
Italy 12

J

Jackson, Henry M. 75, 76, 126
Japan 17, 21–23, 30, 32, 34,
40, 90
John Paul II 8, 100, 113
John XXIII 101, 115
Johnson, Lyndon B. 39, 45
Jones, David C. 59
Jordan 15
Just war 104, 105, 112

K

Kaiser, Karl 82, 83
Kennan, George 28, 74, 79, 81,
122, 126, 149, 151, 159
Kennedy, Edward M. 58, 75,
76
Kennedy, John F. 36, 38–43,
60, 68, 81
*Kennedy, Khrushchev and the
Test Ban* 41
Kissinger, Henry 16, 56
Korea, South 15, 18, 28, 29,
61, 153
Krol, John 105, 106
Krushchev, Nikita 15, 36, 37,
41, 43

L

Launch on warning 1
Law of the Sea 66
Law of Naval Warfare 91
Lawyers Alliance for Nuclear
Arms Control (LANAC) 95,
158
Lebanon 3
Leber, George 82
Limited Test Ban Treaty 39
Linkage 64
Lotus decision 91
Luttwak, Edward N. 74

M

MX 1, 47, 59, 61, 73, 157
MacArthur, Douglas 132
Mali 129
Marshall plan 27
Martens clause 92
Marxism 62, 95, 121, 125, 135,
154

Massachusetts Bar Association
95
Massive retaliation 34, 136
Matthiesen, Leroy 107
McCormick, Richard 108, 114
McNamara, Robert 45, 79, 81
Mertes, Alvis 82
Merton, Thomas 143
Military-industrial complex 13,
37
Minuteman 24, 59, 63
Molander, Earl 126, 127
Molander, Roger 126, 127, 135
Morgenthal, Hans 94
Mountbatten, Lord 30
Mozambique 128
Multiple independently targeted
reentry vehicle (MIRV) 30,
44, 53, 60
Mutual assured destruction
(MAD) 45, 47, 114
Mutual balanced force reduc-
tions (MBFR) 83

N
NATO 3, 16, 28, 36, 54, 58,
62, 71, 80–87, 115, 136,
140, 142, 148, 155
Nagasaki 5, 21–23, 30, 31, 45,
90, 91, 95, 103
National Catholic Reporter 112,
117
National Education Association
66
Neutron bomb 1, 30, 74
Nixon, Richard M. 36, 39, 64,
97, 125
Non-proliferation—See
Proliferation

Non-proliferation Treaty 7, 42,
75, 131
Novak, Michael 111
Nuclear Disarmament—Key
Statements of Popes, Bishops, Councils and Churches
117
Nuclear freeze 5, 6, 13, 22, 30,
31, 37, 41, 42, 47, 56–58,
60, 61, 63–68, 70–80, 82,
87–89, 124, 125, 127, 129,
130, 132, 139–41, 143, 144,
146, 148, 151, 155, 156, 159
Nuclear Illusion and Reality 54
*Nuclear War: What's in it for
You?* 126
*Nuclear Weapons and Interna-
tional Law* 89
Nuremberg principles 93, 94

O
O'Connor, John 109
Odeen, Phillip 114
Office of Technology Assess-
ment 24
Open skies 35
Oppenheimer, J. Robert 33
Outer space 49, 122, 138

P
Pacem in terris 101
Pakistan 10, 15
Palestine Liberation Organiza-
tion 145
Paris Accords 22
Pastoral Constitution on the
Church in the Modern World
101
Pax Christi 54, 55, 107, 109,
117

Peaceful Nuclear Explosion 43, 66

Pentagon 38, 43, 47, 60, 62, 72, 74, 75, 77, 95, 106, 120, 140, 142, 144, 152, 159

People's Republic of China 9, 15–17, 29, 34, 40, 84, 85, 92, 128, 129, 136, 145

Permanent Court of International Justice 91

Pershing II 3, 83

Peru 17

Physicians for Social Responsibility 2, 158

Pierre, Andrew J. 12

Pius XII 100

Podhoretz, Norman 126

Poland 61, 88

Polaris 4, 99

Politics of Arms Control 39

Pope, Alexander 139

Poseidon 4, 44, 69

Powers, Francis Gary 37

Pravda 1

Presidential Directive #59 106

Prohibition of the Use of Nuclear and Thermo-Nuclear Weapons 92

Proliferation 28, 29, 75, 96

Q

Quinn, John 107

R

Reagan, Ronald 6, 9, 11, 42, 43, 51, 56–58, 62, 66, 67, 116, 134

Reagan administration 3, 6, 9, 10, 12, 15, 19, 30, 42, 56–59, 63–68, 70, 72–75, 87, 106, 116, 129, 133, 134, 144, 154

Reilly, Daniel 109

Ritter, Joseph 101, 102

Roach, John 107

Rostow, Eugene 57, 61

Rowney, Edward 72

Runcie, Robert 115

Russian and American Capabilities 68

S

SALT I 6, 42, 45–49, 51–54, 58, 59, 64, 71, 76, 122, 131, 141

SALT II 6, 17, 41, 42, 47, 51, 53–58, 63, 64, 66–68, 71, 77, 122, 125, 127, 132, 141

SALT Experience, The 51

Sampson, Anthony 12

SANE 158

SS-11 24

SS-20 83

Saudi Arabia 9

Schell, Jonathan 139

Schultz, Franz-Josef 82

Scoville, Herbert Jr. 4

Seaborg, Glenn 41

Shimoda case 90, 91, 93

Smith, Gerard 79, 81

Sojourners 140

Somalia 15, 18, 129

South Africa 156

Stalin, Joseph 27, 34, 124

Stanford Arms Control Group 44
Starodubov, Viktor 147
START 6, 51, 58–60, 63, 66, 68, 72, 77, 98, 116, 132, 141, 147
Stassen, Harold 35
State Department 38, 67, 75
Stealth 59
Stevenson, Adlai 37
Stimson, Henry 21, 26, 28
Stoics 94
Strauss, Lewis 33
Submarine-launched ballistic missiles (SLBM) 4, 44, 69, 70
Sudan 15, 129
Suharto, General 128
Sukarno 16
Syria 18
Symingtion amendment 15

T
Taiwan 156
Talbott, Strobe 53
Teller, Edward 41
Ten-Nation Disarmament Committee 37
Test Ban Treaty 37, 40–43, 60, 64, 131
Theological Studies 108, 115, 117
Thoreau, Henry David 149, 150
Threshold test ban 72
Triad 3, 20
Trident 4, 69, 108
Trident II 4, 5, 59, 73

Truman, Harry S. 21, 22, 26, 29, 33, 34
Truman administration 28
Tunisia 15
Turkey 15

U
Underground testing 40–43
Unilateral disarmament 48, 108–10
United Nations 8, 22, 26, 30, 32–34, 36, 40, 62, 92, 95, 131, 155
UN Special Session on Disarmament 8, 18, 62

V
Vance, Cyrus 9, 17, 51, 52
Vatican II 55, 101–106, 109, 110, 115, 156
Venezuela 10, 15
Vietnam 3, 4, 10, 39, 47, 88, 103, 120, 129, 142, 143, 153, 158
Vietnam, North 18, 22, 64
Vitoria, Francisco de 104

W
War Powers Resolution 96, 97
Warner, John 75, 76, 126
Warsaw Pact 36, 57, 80, 82–87, 148
Watergate 3, 4, 38
Weinberger, Caspar 73
Wiesner, Jerome 42, 68, 134
Will, George 78

Winters, Francis X. 115, 116
Wolfe, Thomas W. 51
World Council of Churches
   100, 114

Y

Yalta 21
Yemen, South 128

Yemen, North 129
Yugoslavia 129
Yzermans, Vincent 107

Z

Zablocki, Clement 72, 76
Zahn, Gordon 113
Zuckerman, Solly 54, 133